*With ease of body blest
and peace of mind . . .*
WILLIAM SOMERVILLE (1675-1742)

For the first time, the most effective methods of *authentic* Asiatic self-healing—their basis scientifically confirmed by a noted Nobel Prize winner—have been translated into 100 simplified, speedy routines. Easily understood step-by-step instructions and over 300 professionally modeled photos will show you how you can rid yourself of common aches and stresses—both physical and emotional.

Self-Therap/Ease actually removes **tensions**—the principal cause of most bodily discomforts—at their source *naturally!*

You will find *every* Self-Relax Routine easy to learn, quick to do, and beneficial. All lessons have been carefully prepared and tested by the authors—both highly qualified practitioners and teachers of Therap/Ease. They have adapted this popular procedure from the classic Far Eastern therapy of Healing by Hand. Professor Willem Einthoven, who won the Nobel Prize in 1924 for the development of the electrocardiograph, had proved the vital presence of tiny electrochemical streams triggering human systems. That fact is the principle of this healing art.

Bonnie Pendleton is the first American fully trained in America in authentic Oriental therapy. She and Betty Mehling—who gave up an important position in journalism for this ancient art—studied and were apprenticed under the Western world's outstanding authority on Asiatic Healing by Hand, Mary Iino. Mary had been taught in Japan by Dr. Jiro Murai, renowned for his 50 years of research and development of this centuries-old technique.

Bonnie Pendleton and Betty Mehling were deeply involved and respected in their field well before the United States became Oriental-healing oriented. Previously, they collaborated in a successful textbook now in classroom use by advanced students of Therap/Ease. They were the only representatives of their branch of the healing arts invited to participate in the 1975 and 1976 Headache Seminars at the Medical Center of the University of California at Los Angeles.

Relax! with Self-Therap/Ease has taken the authors two years to plan and produce. Their thoughtful presentation of this complete course of proven self-helps in one easy-to-understand-and-use book is evident in many unusual features, such as the human figure illustrations and the photos that enable you to check affected areas as you use any Relax Routine.

Most important, *Relax! with Self-Therap/Ease* can help you help yourself to feel better, look younger, increase your energy, and improve your health through natural relaxation!

Relax!
With Self-Therap/Ease™*
A Simple Illustrated Course

Bonnie Pendleton & Betty Mehling

CALIFORNIA PUBLICATIONS
CALABASAS, CALIFORNIA

Copyright ©1976 by Bonnie Pendleton and Betty Mehling

All rights reserved, including the right of reproduction
in whole or in part in any form.

Published in 1990 by California Publications
P.O. Box 8014
Calabasas, CA 91302

Originally published by California Publications, copyright ©1976
by Bonnie Pendleton and Betty Mehling.
Published by Prentice-Hall, Inc. 1984
Re-published by California Publications 1990

Library of Congress Catalog Card No. 76-47233
Library of Congress Cataloging-in-Publication Data
Pendleton, Bonnie.
  Relax! with Self-Therap/Ease
  Includes Index.
  1. Acupressure.   2. Relaxation.   3. Betty Mehling

ISBN 0-917306-01-5

Manufactured in the United Stated of America

12th Printing

To the healers of a hundred generations,

who discovered and taught Nature's ways

of helping humans feel better, sooner,

the authors gratefully dedicate this book.

please note...

RELAX ROUTINES are listed on the next two pages — by Routine Number, Main Subject and Page Number.

BEFORE YOU SELECT the Relax Routine, which you think best fits your needs, it is **most important** that you:

(A) **STUDY EXPLANATION:** *"to feel better, sooner"* on page 161. Be sure you do this **before** you refer to Index Listings of **all** conditions helped by Self-Therap/Ease. By carefully reading this short Introduction **first**, you will more easily find the Relax Routines best suited for you.

(B) LOOK THROUGH **ALL** PAGES in this course-book which refer to your condition. You will see that most **bold-type headlines** include **other** conditions as well as the Main Subject. In "As Nature Intended," beginning on page 19, you will learn how Relax Routines are designed to stimulate **natural healing** chain reactions. These transfers of inner energy free tensions, ease aches and gradually restore normal bodily balances. **One** Relax Routine can relieve seemingly unrelated problems.

contents

contents

BEFORE SELECTING RELAX ROUTINE, please read "to feel better, sooner" on page 161.

contents

BEFORE SELECTING RELAX ROUTINE, please read *"to feel better, sooner"* on page 161.

pioneer practitioner

Under scholarships, Irving Schaffner attended Roosevelt University and the University of Illinois. After graduating with a degree in biochemistry, he studied at the College of Pharmacy of the University of Illinois. Later he became a Research Fellow in Medicine at Chicago Medical School, from which he received his M.D. degree. He interned at the Veterans Administration and Los Angeles County Hospitals, taking his residency training in General Practice and Emergency Medicine.

In the 1950s, he began practice in the rolling Conejo Valley, California, about 50 miles northwest of Los Angeles, when the town of Thousand Oaks had a population of 1,500. Today, it is a city of 100,000. Twenty years ago, the area was known primarily as a location of western movie making and "jungleland."

Young Dr. Schaffner was often called to repair wounds inflicted on trainers, and occasionally visitors, by lions, tigers, and other animals. Once he had to reconstruct a human earlobe, part of which had been chewed off by a zebra. Another time he treated a handler who had been stomped on by an elephant. Early one morning, he was awakened by an urgent call: "Come quick, Doc. The stagecoach overturned!" He was rushed to the Paramount Ranch to treat actors trapped and injured under a tipped-over stagecoach. "It was like reliving the early California days," he reminisces.

In his first years in the Conejo Valley, he sometimes had to deliver babies at home or at his office. One "house call" involved carrying a boy with a fractured arm out of a rugged canyon. After years of driving patients 30 miles to the nearest hospital, Dr. Schaffner founded the first hospital in the area. Today, the city has two modern hospitals, equipped with open-heart surgery, with hyperbaric chambers, kidney dialysis machines, and total body scanners. Dr. Schaffner looks back on his pioneer days with no regret. "There is no substitute for the gratification which comes with hard work," he says.

Presently, Dr. Irving Schaffner is on the board of directors of The Hemophilia Foundation, is an associate professor at Charles Drew Post-Graduate Medical School, and is on the faculty of The Bel-Air School for Medical Assistants. He has served on the Boards of Directors of The Conejo Valley Hospital, The Thousand Oaks Broadcasting Company, The Santa Barbara Committee on Alcoholism, The Conejo Valley School for Neurologically Handicapped, and The Psychiatric Research Institute of Beverly Hills. Dr. Schaffner is a senior federal aviation examiner, and is the area medical examiner for Grumman Aircraft Corporation, The Southern California Edison Company, and The Burroughs Corporation. He has served as medical director for The North American-Rockwell Science Center. Dr. Schaffner has twice received awards for work with The American Cancer Society and has contributed to the medical and scientific literature.

AN OPEN MIND
IN MEDICINE

by Irving Schaffner, M.D.

Two events of my younger days made profound impressions on my professional life. When I was ten, my brother contracted polio. After he was sent home from the hospital, presumably with his legs permanently paralyzed, my parents called in nurses trained in the technique of Sister Kenny—then controversial in the medical field. Thanks to the work of these dedicated nuns, my brother's legs were restored to normal use. It was at that time that I resolved to be a physician *and* to never close my eyes to any helpful method of healing.

In medical school, I was privileged to do research work for five years with Dr. Hugo Rony, former chief of endocrinology at the Northwestern University and Chicago Medical Schools. Investigating problems ranging from hair growth and pigmentation to cancer cell metabolism, we were often confronted with situations necessitating unorthodox approaches. Dr. Rony constantly reminded me to keep an open mind in making evaluations.

In twenty years of practice, I have repeatedly found Dr. Rony's advice invaluable. Procedures that were impractical at first sometimes turned out to be successful.

When Oriental therapy was introduced to Western medicine many scoffed. But when applications of this ancient healing art proved effective in certain cases, American and European doctors became less dogmatic about accepting unfamiliar techniques. Positive results are often achieved by those with *full* understanding and *thorough* training in this field. However, the crash-course practitioners may often cause and compound problems, and their failures discourage others from employing these methods.

At the suggestion of a neighbor whose daughter was relieved of muscle spasms resulting from cerebral palsy, I decided to let Betty Mehling apply her adaptation of an ancient Oriental pressure technique, which she calls Therap/Ease, to a patient who suffered severe migraine attacks for many years. This woman, in her sixties, was taking the drug Caffergot in such large doses that her circulation had become severely impaired. Over the years, she had consulted many physicians, specialists, and nonmedical consultants. Indeed, she had even had her uterus removed on the advice of the psychic Edgar Cayce. But even after the hysterectomy, her disabling headaches continued. On several occasions, I was summoned to her home to administer intravenous medication. This was truly a stubborn case.

To my surprise, when next I saw my patient after a month of Therap/Ease treatments, I found her circulation much improved; she had been able to cut down the Caffergot medication, yet her headaches had been markedly reduced in frequency and severity. This success was repeated with several patients—those with migraine and musculo-skeletal disorders. But I was really convinced that Therap/Ease, as developed and practiced by Betty Mehling and Bonnie Pendleton, merits consideration when my wife, who had suffered for two years following a severe cervical whiplash injury, obtained more relief from Therap/Ease treatments than from other modalities previously used on her, including cortisone injections, traction, hot packs, massages, ultrasound, and Diathermy.

Therap/Ease is simple, harmless, and yields a high rate of positive results. Perhaps our Western-trained therapists, after testing some of the Therap/Ease techniques, can adopt those procedures they find most useful in their own practices. After all, an open mind is the key to learning.

understanding physician

Examinations and tests seldom frighten patients of Dr. Alfred Mekelburg. His always-cheerful manner reduces anxieties at once. His patients tell friends and relatives that somehow pain seems to lessen even before medical treatment. That's one reason why two and now three generations of families in the huge San Fernando Valley of Southern California depend, with surety, on his care.

Dr. Mekelburg's comforting attitude is part of his positive philosophy of the practice of medicine. However deeply he is concerned about a patient's condition or how much he is inwardly affected by the problems of the preceding visit, there is no indication of doubt in his look or his tone.

Alfred Mekelburg, who graduated from and later taught at the Tufts University School of Medicine and served his residency at The New England Medical Center in Boston, firmly believes in improved, compassionate treatment of human ills. He demonstrated this as a naval surgeon in World War II and the Korean War. He is a Fellow of The American Academy of Family Practice and a most important part of a Pain Control Clinic team. He serves as consultant in his field to his colleagues.

HEALING OF TENSIONS

by Alfred Mekelburg, M.D.

When I first heard about Therap/Ease, I was not particularly impressed. A friend whose minor aches and stresses following an accident had somehow been quickly relieved was enthusiastic about Oriental therapy; adding that this method eased other tensions. I was even less interested in that.

This negative approach is opposite to my usual attitude. Unfortunately, as a family physician, I have heard—often with disgust—of what are claimed to be sure cures for serious illnesses. Quacks who are both greedy and vicious hold their unlucky victims with continued false hopes; often until it is too late for qualified professional help. Too many lives have been needlessly sacrificed this way.

That is why I was, and am, skeptical of any technique without satisfactory proof of its effectiveness.

A few weekends later, I became a victim of severe whiplash. By coincidence, the next day I saw the same friend. With my usual heavy work load scheduled for the days ahead, I mentioned that my taking time off for traction and wearing a padded collar could have unfavorable psychological effects on my patients.

It was a Sunday evening. "Therap/Ease will help, I'm sure," my friend said. Before I could object, a call had been made and an immediate appointment with Bonnie Pendleton had been arranged.

Under the circumstances, it seemed worth a trial. After three one-hour sessions, all discomforts connected with the whiplash injury, along with a couple of tensions in other parts of my neck, had completely disappeared.

Physiologically, I was aware of what Mrs. Pendleton was doing. Areas where she placed her fingers, with one hand stationary while the other was moved every few minutes until another routine replaced the former, were not only parts of the neck, skull, and upper back affected by the strained muscles. Other locations distant from the neck, particularly in the lumbar region, were involved. Nerve tensions caused by the accident were relieved. Dislocated parts returned to normal positions without any forceful adjustment. I was over the whiplash.

Now I *was* impressed. Any doubts I had left about use of this form of treatment for tension-related muscular difficulties were gone after every patient of mine I referred to Bonnie Pendleton was helped. Long discussions with her convinced me that routines used by her and Betty Mehling, both trained by an authentic Oriental-therapy specialist, accomplished natural healing without exaggerated claims. There is a definite need for the Self-Therap/Ease exercises they have developed.

Therap/Ease is certainly a proven, ethical healing art. Like Acupuncture as practiced by physician specialists, this manual therapy has empirical qualities. Science has not yet analyzed how or why these treatments bring such beneficial results. Therefore, it must be considered an empirical remedy.

The total fund of medical information is by no means complete at this time. Therefore, I keep my mind open to all new as well as old methods that have proven themselves, including empirical treatments.

My experience, as well as the experiences of my referred patients relieved by Therap/Ease, induced me to an in-depth study of Oriental medicine.

I am confident that many others have had distressing aches alleviated by Therap/Ease. The reader can also help himself or herself through *Relax! with Self-Therap/Ease.*

Alfred Mekelburg MD

How *Relax!* with *Self-Therap/Ease*™ Came to Be

Most Americans were unaware of Far Eastern methods of medicine until the early 1970s when a Washington newswriter reported from China about the effective use of acupuncture as an anesthetic. Widespread publicity of this specialized Oriental technique followed.

We who had been active in Asiatic therapy in this country were delighted when this information broke through. Opening the door to proven therapeutics had been long overdue. For many years, suppression on both sides of the Pacific had kept the knowledge of natural Healing by Hand out of general Western use.

Two consequences of the publicity were, however, of concern to those of us engaged in Eastern therapy—professionals, students, and the many Americans who had been helped by this healing art. Feature stories dramatized acupuncture, a complicated procedure practiced only by highly trained surgeons and physicians. Those who were attracted by the newspaper reports would think that acupuncture is all there is to Asiatic healing. But we can learn to use hands—a normal instinct—before trying to master control of tools or instruments. Acupuncture, the most involved offshoot of natural Healing by Hand, is excellent for relief of unusually severe conditions when administered by specialists. Over 500 points of deep piercing have to be understood in this intricate study.

Acupuncture and similarly named derivatives, such as osteopuncture, are also expensive. Only very stubborn cases are referred to these specialists. However, there is no piercing of skin in Self-Therap/Ease, which uses 28 Power Centers to relieve tensions throughout the entire body. Ordinarily, only four to six Power Centers are used to get meaningful results in a Relax Routine.

Many recently published books presenting Oriental therapies featured involved procedures. Such introduction to a highly beneficial art was certainly not fair to beginners who were seeking simple, yet well-founded, help. It was like trying to teach first-grade children arithmetic by presenting trigonometry. Or trying to teach a student driver how to drive a huge seven-speed tractor pulling two trailers instead of teaching him how to drive a car first. In addition, disseminating unqualified material harms the respected reputations of fine practitioners of Oriental healing who have been helping and teaching thousands of Americans before the public was bombarded by takeoffs on acupuncture.

The second concern was expressed by people who had been relieved of tensions and aches by Therap/Ease. It has been our practice for years to give those we help some "healthwork." These simple between-sessions self-treatments speed relief and help maintain normal bodily balances. These people had hoped that in the flood of books based on Oriental therapy, they would find easy-to-understand self-helps such as we had recommended.

Some of the new books, particularly those by well-trained Oriental practitioners, are informative to professionals. But the contents could be confusing to those unfamiliar with human physiology and bodily functions. Other books omitted or failed to explain the importance of specific *combinations* of Power Centers. These bases of most *effective* therapy are stressed in authentic Asiatic healing techniques and are included in both acupuncture and Therap/Ease.

We realized the need to spread a basic knowledge of the uses and advantages of modified Asiatic self-therapy. And we are aware that the demand for teachers of Therap/Ease far exceeds the present supply.

More than two years of planning, thinking, and design went into changing Therap/Ease to self-treatments, making preliminary sketches of positions of models before the photography, simplifying, writing, rewriting, and re-rewriting, until the clearest possible instructions and illustrations were attained.

The 100 Relax Routines in this book are proven-effective Self-Therap/Ease treatments, illustrated and explained for quick understanding.

as nature intended

healing yourself—inner and outer

Nature designed your marvelous body to serve you efficiently for many years. To assure normal continuity of vital functions, self-maintenance and self-healing systems were built into you. These automatic protectors include reserves of eyesight and other faculties, antibodies, blood-clotting, separate brain flows, and a variety of shock absorbers and equalizers. Your most important self-healer of minor systemic problems is *natural rest!*

Relaxed sleep removes pent-up stresses and related aches. Proper rest revitalizes elements of life, corrects inner imbalances, and regains depleted strength and mental composure. The main cause of most human discomforts, unrest, lack of vigor, and even facial lines is *not* aging. It is *tension!*

Tensions tie up muscles and nerves as the result of injury, neglect, illness, or emotion. Muscles and nerves are fed by energy. Thus, stresses not only can cause aches, they can also reduce vitality and interfere with peace of mind.

The first aim of this course is to teach you to *relax,* quickly and naturally. Self-Therap/Ease will show you how easily you can activate your *relax* self-healers. As this is accomplished, you will direct your built-in protectors to make needed repairs. The main goal of Self-Therap/Ease is to return *all* your functions to normal operation. As a result, *true* relaxation will soothe your body and mind, as well as your facial expression.

Your well-being is in *your* hands! Your hands and the basic knowledge of how to use your self-healers to your advantage are all you need to remove bothersome tensions at their *source* and to rid your inner self of common conditions—just as Nature intended!

how this course
can help you help yourself

Therap/Ease is not a new idea! We have merely translated into clear English the most valuable, improved factors of authentic Asiatic Healing by Hand—the natural therapy with the longest successful record. For thousands of years, these simple methods have eased many conditions in millions of Far Eastern people. For over twenty years, this effective art has been increasing in use in this country. Thousands of Americans have been relieved of tensions and connected problems naturally and safely.

The basis of Therap/Ease—and Healing by Hands—electrochemical energy related to human physiology—was scientifically substantiated by

19

Willem Einthoven in 1903. Professor Einthoven was awarded the Nobel Prize in 1924 for his invention of the electrocardiograph, using the same principle of transfer of minute electrical currents.

Self-Therap/Ease is a further simplification of this technique. Methods of self-relief of most common discomforts are included in the 100 Relax Routines in this book. Each series of patterns has been conscientiously planned and thoroughly tested and proven. Plain instructions illustrated with step-by-step photos make helping yourself easy and interesting, as well as beneficial.

To feel and look better just select the Relax Routine specifically designed to relieve your discomfort. Following these three guides will speed results:

1. Read this and the following pages of explanation to understand *why* and *how* these procedures work.
2. Before you choose the Relax Routine to fit your need, study the paragraph: "To Feel Better Sooner," on page 161. These important facts can save you much time and effort.
3. For the first week, once daily, start your self-treatments with Relax Routine 1. Then proceed *immediately* with the Relax Routine you have selected to ease your condition. You will find the reasons for beginning with this temporary preliminary in "For Openers" on page 33.

you and your wonders

Among the marvelous processes in your inner self are the steps that change what you eat, drink, and breathe into your body's fuels. Abuses of this system, such as overindulgence, bring indigestion, headache, nausea, diarrhea, and constipation. Most of these problem signals can be traced to tensions along the route of the process. Your body lets you know when it is being abused.

Another fascinating inner wonder is the intricate network of tiny currents, known in Asiatic healing as "energy flows." These miniature streams of power are integral parts of your nerve-and-muscle system and cover every inch of your body. Nature so located energy flows to insure normal functions, internally and externally. Your electrochemistry can affect your appearance as well as your disposition.

These tiny conductors of bodily power control notify you when any of your systems are not operating within allowable limits. A headache, for example, warns you of an abnormal condition in—or possibly distant from—your head.

Besides your five *outer* senses, you have many more *inner* communicators. Blockages in energy flows usually are felt at intersections of two or more power streams. These areas of sensitivity are called Power Centers. As shown in the photos on pages 30 and 31 and as shaded parts of figure illustrations on pages 168 to 171, most Power Centers are easy to reach. When any of these areas are painful rather than just sensitive to your touch, congestion is nearby. This discomfort is Nature's warning of excess tension in these flows.

As a road accident can cause traffic to slow up or stop blocks away, congestion in energy flows often affects distant parts of your body. You know that headaches are not always caused by problems in the skull. Sinus, tooth, eye, or ear disorders can be responsible. But headaches can also signal warnings from other areas. Faulty digestion or elimination, general tensions or fatigue, or other abnormalities or imbalances elsewhere in your system can be the problem. There may also be what are called "referred" pains.

Consider the size and hardness of the calf-muscle knot when a "charleyhorse" is suffered. Observe how neck arteries and veins swell in an excited person. These are *visible* distortions. Imagine what happens to your inner muscles under physical or mental strain. Tensions tighten flexible muscles. Tiny paths of energy—so all-important to your well-being—are impaired by stretched muscles and taut nerves.

Whenever possible, nature repairs malfunctions in its processes. Relaxed rest, when available, is a helpful remedy. Often, connected pain may make *natural* sleep unattainable. Sometimes, depending on the cause and severity of tension, obstructions may remain *after* rest. Continued aches keep stealing energy. Combining Self-Therap/Ease with rest usually expedites return of normal flows. In many common conditions, Therap/Ease restores proper functions with no more rest than the time of self-treatments. Relief of deep or long-lasting problems will obviously take longer. That is why starting Self-Therap/Ease *as soon as* you feel discomfort or increased sensitivity in Power Centers is very important!

natural healing at the source

Just *when* people became aware of their self-healing properties or how they began soothing their discomforts is not known. Putting hands to hurts is intuitive. Crude self-treatments often help. Warmth of the hands along with haphazard transfer of minuscule electrochemical energy can temporarily ease minor aches or small strains. With growing respect for Nature's foresight, use of hands for healing was undoubtedly included in the Master Plan of human intelligence and self-care.

We do know *where* natural healing developed into a logically based art rather than hit-or-miss voodoo. It was in China. And twentieth-century American medical doctors have witnessed techniques related to true Asiatic therapy used by American Indians. Members of two tribes stated that they were following procedures handed down from their ancestors from one generation to the next. Anthropologists have theorized that Indians came to the Western hemisphere from Asia over the former Aleutian land bridge about 20,000 years ago.

Medicine men were called shamans by both American Indians and Asians. We are indebted to groups of Chinese shamans for the benefits of

Oriental therapy that are helping thousands of Americans today. Claiming priestly abilities of healing bodies and minds, many shamans served families of political leaders. This was long before any organized religion. The practical warlords were not satisfied with the priests' blaming their failures to heal tensions on the wrongdoings of the patient's ancestors. So the shamans began to take this aspect of their duties more seriously.

Instinctively, they firmly held the hurts of deeply rooted muscular tensions. After short discomfort, this brought some relief. They extended pressure to surrounding areas. They attained further results.

Moving their fingers from one tender spot to another, the shaman healers noted paths, similar in all individuals, that were somehow involved with the sensitive areas. There was a direct relationship between pain and energy. As aches increased in intensity, natural vigor decreased. They learned to call the affected paths "energy flows." That was during the Hsia Dynasty. When Abraham was launching a new concept of religion in the Middle East, a new idea in natural therapy—Healing by Hand—was being organized in the Far East.

Patiently, generation after generation, the early experimenters passed along their findings. After many trials, they found that pressing on two related spots at the same time achieved relief that was much longer lasting than working on one point at a time. This true approach to relaxation—correct combinations—is the basis of Therap/Ease and acupuncture, as authentic adaptations of original Oriental therapy.

About 3500 years ago—around the time of Moses—the Shang Dynasty encouraged the dissemination of knowledge in China. Since paper, permanent black ink, and camels' hair brushes were already in use in that country, all major events were recorded. When researching events before the Roman Empire, modern scientists and historians depend on two sources: the Old Testament and the Chinese Books of Bamboo, dating back to that period.

Teams of specialists in Healing by Hand explored the mysteries of vital inner paths. They found muscles near the surface that relayed tensions from deeper locations. They felt that Nature had so arranged problem areas for convenient treatment. They traced energy flows, located most essential holding spots in these paths, and began to discover self-healers. They proved that the most effective way to relieve tensions is by holding *two related key points*. These techniques were the foundation of preventive medicine. The Asiatic practice of paying the doctor only as long as the patient stays well is still in use in the Far East.

The early Orientals sensed our inner forces but could not explain them scientifically. Through finding two-way paths within us, they anticipated Harvey's discovery of blood circulation, with the heart as a two-way pump, by 3,000 years. Without understanding a more mysterious element, they learned how to use it to advantage. Einthoven's breakthrough in discovering electrochemical energy confirmed the ancient Chinese findings. This infinitesimal current triggers our heartbeats as an inbuilt pacemaker and is meant to regulate much of our physiology.

After several hundred years in China, the therapy spread to Japan. Practitioners and innovations and improvements in techniques were exchanged between the two countries. Civil wars in China made Japan—for a few centuries—the leader in developing refinements of diagnosis and methods of teaching.

Self-Therap/Ease is the first course of systematized self-helps that includes the best features of both Chinese and Japanese procedures. Only advanced technicalities have been omitted.

In one way, you may compare your involved energy flows to the circuit breakers in the electrical wiring of your home. When a circuit is overloaded, the breaker shuts off current to areas served by connected wiring. Our personal power systems must be kept going every second of every minute 24 hours every day! Instead of shutoff (except in unusually drastic tensions, such as strokes), we are warned by taut feelings and sometimes by pain to attend to the condition. By motivating connected energy flows, a chain reaction will relax *all* bodily tensions.

The Relax Routines designed to ease your condition, used *regularly,* will thus eliminate congestions throughout your systems and restore energy flows to normal balance. Self-Therap/Ease applied as directed will correct minor conditions before they can become major problems. These self-treatments are established *facts,* not fads.

Your well-being is truly in your hands! Put them to work for *you . . . now!*

a "third hand"

Towel Knot or Rubber Ball As Self-Therap/Ease Tools

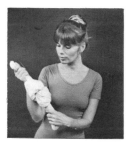
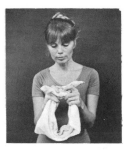

A hand towel, knotted as illustrated, or a sponge-rubber ball can be doubly effective as a "third hand" for use on back areas otherwise hard to reach. By this means, you will also add benefits of a third point of contact, to expedite unblocking of congestions in energy paths.

Be sure to **combine** placement of towel knot or ball with **positions** of your **hands,** as directed in routines where these "third hands" are included. Find the most sensitive spot within the darkened areas on the small back photo, above Relax Routine instructions.

How Towels Are Used

Tie a simple single knot in a hand towel. Either lie flat on the towel knot placed under sensitive area, as illustrated, or, if you prefer, lean back against towel knot as you sit in a chair.

Use of Rubber Ball

A sponge-rubber ball about 2½ inches in diameter may be substituted for a towel knot—except on bony areas where a ball may bruise skin or bone. (A rubber ball cut in half and put flat-side down on floor or bed will be easier to handle and will not roll out of position.) Sponge-rubber balls have been found to be the most effective in lying down or reclining positions (as in a dentist's chair or airplane seat) when one's own body weight creates the pressure.

reversing relax routines

For your easier understanding, most Relax Routines are designed, worded, and illustrated to show you how to attain relief for *either* Left or Right side of your body, limbs, or head. If instructions and photographs for *both* Left *and* Right sides were printed, confusion would result. This has been proven by many prepublication tests.

Please read the description beginning "Illustrated Routine..." under the conditions that are written in boldface type before proceeding.

Just remember that this description will let you know whether Left or Right side is shown by the photos and hand-position instructions that follow. If the side illustrated is the area you want helped, just use your hands as directed.

To relieve the opposite side, simply *reverse* the Routine. Just switch Lefts to Rights and Rights to Lefts.

You will note in preliminary descriptions that a few Relax Routines should *not* be reversed.

For best overall results, *always reverse* procedure *if so instructed* at the end of routine. Even though you seem to be more uncomfortable on *one* side, correcting imbalances or obstructions on *both* sides will speed the chain reaction Nature intended to help your entire body.

examples of reversing routines

A-1 *Right* hand holds *Left* side of neck and *Left* hand holds under *Right* collarbone. *Reverse instructions,* so that in

A-2 *Left* hand holds *Right* side of neck and *Right* hand holds under *Left* collarbone.

B-1 shows towel knot under *Right* lower shoulder-blade area, *Right* hand under *Right* waist and *Left* hand holding *Right* side of neck, *Reverse instructions* so that in

B-2 towel knot is under *Left* lower shoulder-blade area, *Left* hand is under *Left* waist and *Right* hand holds *Left* side of neck.

don't diagnose yourself!

Ask yourself: "**How** am I?" *Why* you feel any way but normal can best be answered by the skills and experiences of a physician and by results of tests.

We have seen, both in and out of doctors' offices, breakdowns of health brought on by unwise and incorrect self-diagnoses and treatments. We have witnessed tragedies caused by fears—often unnecessary—of facing the truth. Other serious problems were traced to irresponsible opinions of quacks offering false claims of cures. Many illnesses would not become serious if a physician's advice had been promptly sought and followed. No single treatment, diet, or medication can be a cure for all ailments.

Please do not assume that because these self-treatments are based on the longest-known effective natural healing art that they can substitute for examination and diagnosis by a qualified physician.

Self-Therap/Ease can supplement your doctor's treatment, to reduce his office work load. You may ask your doctor to specify Relax Routines to ease your discomforts due to minor imbalances he or she finds in your system. Medical journals report significant increases in the number of physicians referring patients to this form of therapy.

If your condition is caused by muscular or emotional tensions, you can be assured that you can in *no way harm yourself* by using any of the 100 Relax Routines. If, however, you are not sure of the cause of your aches or pains, please do not take chances with your health! For example, tightness in the chest may merely signal a beginning symptom of an ordinary cold. In that case, Relax Routines indexed under "Colds, Chest" can alleviate the pressure. But continued or sudden pains in the chest area may warn you of a much more serious condition. Such problems require immediate medical attention.

Please don't consider *Relax! With Self-Therap/Ease* a guess-my-ailment game! A thorough physical checkup will clear up your doubts. Then help yourself to relief of common complaints by following the simple *Self*-Therap/Ease course to *Relax!*

for quicker understanding

Follow the guidelines on pages 30 and 31, and in minutes you'll be able to rid yourself of strains and stresses.

Study photos of the Power Centers. They represent the holding areas included in *all* 100 Relax Routines. You will find the same captions designating the 28 Self-Therap/Ease Power Centers on the full-figure illustrations on pages 168 to 171.

Relax! with Self-Therap/Ease has been planned to help you achieve quicker, easier self-healing. You don't have to memorize locations of the Power Centers. They are photographed on pages 30 and 31 and illustrated on pages 168 to 171.

With **Self**-Therap/Ease *you* must select your self-treatment Relax Routines. Based on your description of your discomfort, a practical therapist with qualified Therap/Ease training would *know* what Relax Routines to use. Guiding you to easy selection of the *correct* Relax Routine was our biggest challenge in translating practitioner knowledge and experience into simple self-helps. The practical, **easy-to-understand** procedure we developed is the result of many trials.

Please turn to page 161. *"To feel better, sooner,"* is your **key** to finding the **right** Relax Routine for **your** self-treatment. That paragraph will show you how to choose the Relax Routine that is best for **you.**

BACK OF BODY

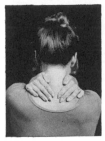

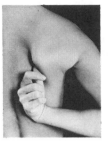
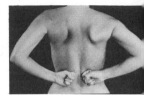

WAIST

UPPER SHOULDER
BLADE AREA

MIDDLE SHOULDER
BLADE AREA

LOWER SHOULDER
BLADE AREA

LEG AND FOOT

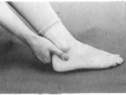
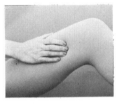
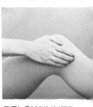

OUTSIDE UPPER
CALF

BELOW OUTER
ANKLEBONE

INNER THIGH

BELOW INNER
KNEE

FRONT OF BODY

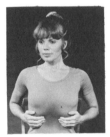

GROIN

UNDER
COLLARBONE

UPPER BREAST

INNER RIB CAGE

HEAD

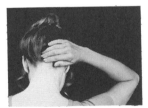

L & R BASES OF SKULL

CENTER BASE
OF SKULL

SIDE OF NECK

SINCE EVERY BODY is different, individual areas of sensitivity vary. To locate
your exact Power Centers, just find the most tender spot in those particular area
These spots are **always** to be held in **combination**.

OWER CENTERS

ton and Betty Mehling

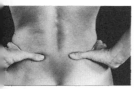

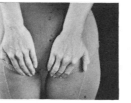

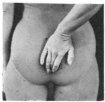

CK OF HIP

BUTTOCK

TAILBONE

OTOGRAPHS show close-up individual views of Power Centers, illustrated in shaded areas on figures on cover extensions.

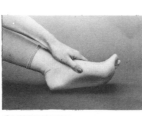

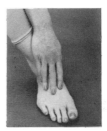

ELOW INNER
NKLEBONE

OUTER EDGE
OF ARCH

TOP OF FOOT

ARM

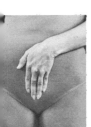

BIC BONE

INNER ELBOW

INSIDE
UPPER ARM

OUTER SHOULDER
BLADE AREA

FACE

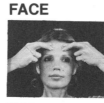

BONE BEHIND EAR

FOREHEAD

UNDER CHEEKBONE

EXCEPT tailbone, pubic bone and center base of head, all Power Centers listed are located on **both Right** and **Left** ides of body.

for true relaxation,
free of tensions and aches,
just follow these rules...

1. **THIS IS IMPORTANT!** Read **again: "to feel better, sooner"** on page 161. Decide **what** Relax Routines (first and second choices) best fit your needs. Study wording and photos on Routines involved — **BEFORE YOU BEGIN!**

2. **FOR THE FIRST WEEK,** start your self-treatments with Relax Routine 1. Your advantages in "warm-up" are explained in *"for openers,"* next page. **IMMEDIATELY AFTER** completing Relax Routine 1, proceed with Routine selected.

3. IF YOU NEED RELIEF on the same side (Left or Right), as illustrated in Relax Routine, go ahead! Should your problem be on the **other** side, REVERSE ROUTINE, as on page 26.

4. PLACE YOUR HANDS (and — if directed — towel knot or sponge-rubber ball) in positions shown. Press most sensitive spot in the area. Locations of tender points vary in individuals.

5. **ALWAYS USE BOTH HANDS** (and towel knot or ball) at **same time!** Self-Therap/Ease **combinations** speed relief.

6. MAINTAIN FIRM PRESSURE. For the first few self-treatments, accumulated tensions will likely make affected areas tender to your hold. Regular use of Relax Routines will remove the sensitivity, and eliminate causes of tension tenderness — *at the source.*

NOTE: If several Self-Therap/Ease treatments, carefully selected and preceded by Relax Routine 1, do not relieve your condition, you should consult a physician.

reminder...

WHEN should Relax Routines be used? Whether your problem is of long duration, or you've just begun to feel it — start Self-Therap/Ease **at once!** The sooner you start, the sooner you'll feel results! And the less chance of the tension or ache developing into a serious situation.

SELF-THERAP/EASE is a **preventive** as well as **corrective** healing art. Self-treatments designed to relieve and control bothersome conditions should be continued **regularly.** Severe problems often require two or three repeats of Relax Routines daily until eased. After that, or in cases of mild discomforts, Self-Therap/Ease once a day will bring continued relaxation and relief of common pains.

TIME RECOMMENDED for each step in Routines is minimum. Devote **as much time** as you find helpful. Self-Therap/ Ease can not harm you.

for openers...

TO HELP START a gasoline engine which has been inactive, raw fuel (choke) is usually needed. A similar preliminary step will relieve tensions sooner. Relax Routine 1, as a warm-up exercise, will make your first Self-Therap/Ease treatments more effective. Tensions caused by injury or long neglect often accumulate in areas other than where you may feel the most stress. Relax Routine 1 will begin to break up such trouble-making obstructions in energy flows.

FOR THE FIRST WEEK, once daily, start your self-treatments with Relax Routine 1 (next two pages) immediately **before** you use the Relax Routine you have selected to ease your condition. This will bring you over-all relaxation sooner.

relax

**Relieves bodily tensions…simple backaches…hives.
Restores energy. Eases throat hoarseness.**

Illustrated routine will help *ENTIRE* body.

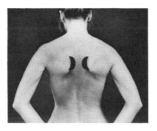

Lie on 2 towel knots,
or sponge rubber balls,
one under each mid-shoulder
blade area.

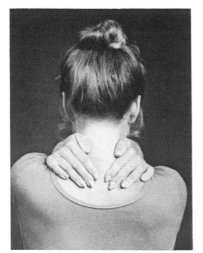

Illustrated to show positions of hands.

(A) Press both Right
and Left upper shoulder
blade areas. Cross arms, if
more comfortable. Lie down.

TIME: 3 minutes

---

please remember…

RELAX ROUTINE 1 IS ALSO **"for openers."**
*While you will find this Routine an excellent
9-minute over-all Relaxer, at any time — this
procedure is especially beneficial to begin helping
your self with SELF-THERAP/EASE.*

(B) Place fists, knuckles up, at
     each side of spine under waist.

TIME: 3 minutes

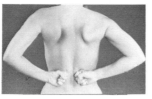

BACK VIEW

(C) Lie on hands, palms down,
     under back of hips.

  TIME: 3 minutes

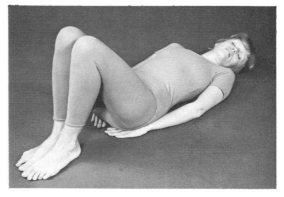

PLEASE TURN TO PAGE 161. *"To feel
better, sooner,"* is your **KEY** to finding the
right Relax Routine for **your** self-treatment.
That paragraph will show you how to choose
Routine best for **you.**

relax

Relieves general tensions. Stimulates energy.

Illustrated routine will help *LEFT* side.
To relieve *RIGHT* side, *REVERSE ROUTINE.*

Right hand presses Left upper shoulder blade area.

Place Right foot on inside area of Left knee.
(Use pillow under Right knee, if desired.)

Left thumb presses each Left fingernail for one minute.

TIME: 4 minutes

REVERSE ROUTINE

AMONG RELAX ROUTINES, you will find messages from people who have effectively used these procedures to help themselves to relaxation and better health. Number of Relax Routine used by the individual follows each testimonial. While those named have found specified routines helpful in easing *their* tensions and aches, and in restoring *their* energies...please remember that discomforts in one area can have more than one cause.

YOU MAY FIND other Relax Routines more effective for your self than those numbered to relieve *your* particular problem. You are urged to read carefully the message on page 161, as well as *all* conditions headlined in *all* related Relax Routines listed in the Index.

relax

Relieves tension discomforts of legs and feet.

Illustrated routine will help RIGHT side.
To relieve LEFT side, REVERSE ROUTINE.

Illustration shows positions
of hands.

Right thumb holds
under Right knee.

Left hand holds middle
bottom of Right foot.

TIME: 3 minutes

REVERSE ROUTINE

This routine is as effective
in lying position, if preferred.

relax

Relieves upper arm and chest tensions.

Illustrated routine will help *LEFT* side.
To relieve *RIGHT* side, *REVERSE ROUTINE.*

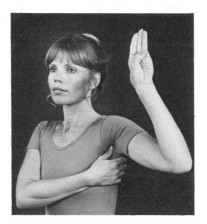

(A) Right thumb presses
into Left armpit.

Left thumb presses nail
of Left little finger.

TIME: 3 minutes

Self-Therap/Ease relieved discomfort in my ankles with a Relax Routine. But as I don't accept anything with just one trial, I considered a longer-lasting problem. Since I was 18, fatigue had brought a numbness in my right shoulder and right arm. A physician diagnosed this as a pinched nerve. When I discussed this with Betty Mehling, she suggested this simple routine. As soon as the symptom becomes apparent, this procedure eliminates the numbness for long periods.
ROBERT STEINMETZ Ph.D. (Educational Psychologist)
Woodland Hills, California

Relax Routine 4

relax

(B) Right hand stays as in (A).

    Left hand presses gently
    upward under
    Right collarbone.

TIME: 3 minutes

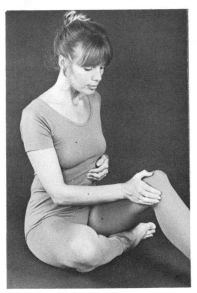

(C) Right hand holds below Left
    inner knee.

    Cup Left fingers firmly around
    Left inner rib cage.

TIME: 3 minutes

REVERSE ROUTINE

This routine is as effective
in lying position, if preferred.

relax

Relieves shoulder tensions. Restores energy.

Illustrated routine will help *RIGHT* side.
To relieve *LEFT* side, *REVERSE ROUTINE.*

Left hand presses Right upper shoulder blade area.

Right thumb presses Right fingernails, one at a time, for one minute each.

TIME: 4 minutes

REVERSE ROUTINE

This routine is as effective in lying position, if preferred.

Much pressure develops in my upper back and shoulder area, from my leaning over a typewriter at work. When I asked Betty Mehling for self-treatments to relieve these tensions, she recommended this Relax Routine for 4 to 5 minutes on each side. This always helps me. In fact, I now use it as a twice-daily relaxing routine AT MY DESK!

PATSY GIBBS (Assistant Editor)
Hermosa Beach, Calif.

Relax Routine 5

relax

Relieves tensions in neck and back.

Illustrated routine will help *LEFT* side.
To relieve *RIGHT* side, *REVERSE ROUTINE.*

Place towel knot under
Left mid-shoulder blade area.

If seated position is substituted,
added benefits of use of towel
knot would be lost.

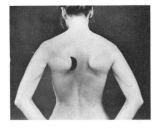

(A) Place Left fist under Right
waist. In seated position,
leaning back into fist
increases effectiveness.

Right hand holds Left side
of neck firmly.

TIME: 3 minutes

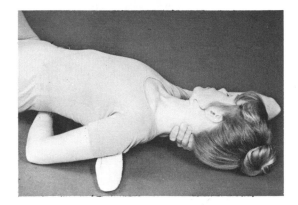

(B) Left hand presses into
Right groin.

Right hand presses Left
upper shoulder blade area.

TIME: 3 minutes

**REVERSE ROUTINE AND
TOWEL-KNOT POSITION.**

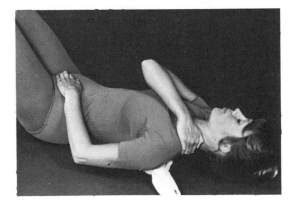

41

back

Relieves lower back tensions...tired legs.

Illustrated routine will help *ENTIRE* body, including both legs.

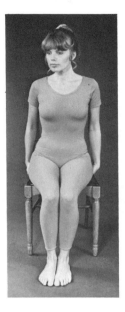

Sit with hands under
Right and Left buttocks.

TIME: 3 minutes
(or as long as you feel at ease.)

Sitting on upholstered chair, or on
carpeted floor, is recommended
for comfort.

*Within minutes of my using this easy routine, tensions leave
my lower back. Along with this stress, which had bothered
me for years, I have lost the anxiety of the condition recur-
ring. If it should bother me again I have the double comfort
of knowing I can help myself — without depending on pills.*

MADELAINE CRANE (Artist)
Sepulveda, Calif.

Relax Routine 7

back

Eases upper and middle back tensions.
Reduces abdominal bloat.

Illustrated routine will help LEFT side.
To relieve RIGHT side, REVERSE ROUTINE.

Place towel knot under Left mid-shoulder blade area.

If seated position is substituted, added benefits of use of towel knot would be lost.

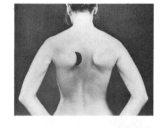

(A) Place Right fist under Left waist. In seated position, leaning back into fist increases effectiveness.

Left hand presses Right inner thigh.

TIME: 3 minutes

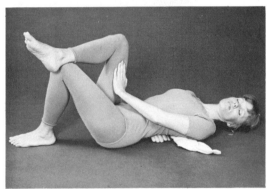

(B) Right fist stays as in (A).

Left hand holds outside Right upper calf.

TIME: 3 minutes

**REVERSE ROUTINE AND
TOWEL-KNOT POSITION.**

43

back

Relieves general backaches...bladder discomforts... cramps in muscles of knee and calf (charleyhorse).

Illustrated routine will help *LEFT* side.
To relieve *RIGHT* side, *REVERSE ROUTINE.*

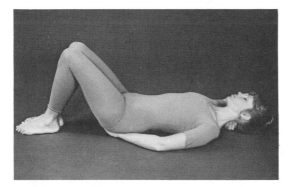

(A) Right hand holds Left side of neck firmly.

Place Left hand under tailbone, palm up or down, whichever is more comfortable.

TIME: 3 minutes

I am so thankful for the self-helps to which Bonnie Pendleton introduced me. These Relax Routines have relieved various conditions. Every morning, before I do any chores at Hilltop Ranch, I do this simple exercise. That is why I'm able to feel as well as I do, and to be so active.

PEGGY BROOKS (Rancher)
Sunland, Calif.

Relax Routine 9

(B) Right hand stays as in (A).

Left thumb holds back of
Left knee.

TIME: 3 minutes

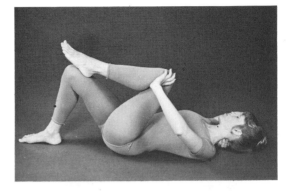

(C) Right hand stays as in (A).

Left thumb holds below
outer Left anklebone.

TIME: 3 minutes

REVERSE ROUTINE

This routine is as effective
in seated position, if preferred.

head

**Eases common headaches...dizziness...
discomforts of head colds.
Relieves eye tensions...stomach queasiness.**

Illustrated routine will help *ENTIRE* body and head.

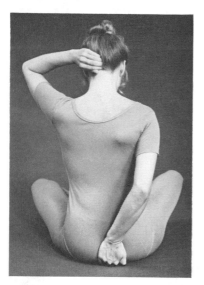

(A) Place Right hand under
     tailbone, palm up or down,
     whichever is
     more comfortable.

     Left hand presses Center
     base of head.

TIME: 3 minutes

(B) Right hand stays as in (A).

     Left thumb presses between
     eyes gently.

TIME: 3 minutes

46

(C) Right hand stays as in (A).

Place Left hand between breasts, fingers pointing downward.

TIME: 3 minutes

(D) Right hand stays as in (A).

Left hand presses pubic bone.

TIME: 3 minutes

This routine is equally effective in either lying or seated position.

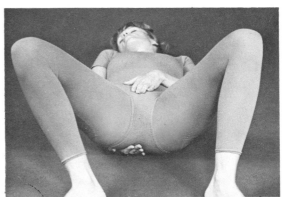

head

Relieves side-of-head pains...eyestrain...side-of-leg tensions...tailbone discomforts.

Illustrated routine will help *LEFT* side-of-head and *RIGHT* side-of-leg tensions. To relieve *RIGHT* side-of-head and *LEFT* side-of-leg, *REVERSE ROUTINE.*

(A) Right hand presses bone behind Left ear.

Left hand holds Right forehead firmly.

TIME: 3 minutes

When my wife started talking about the relief she was getting from Self-Therap/Ease, I thought it was mostly psychological. However, after getting relief myself from a long-standing sinus headache condition, I also became a booster.

DEAN SNELL (Engineer)
Pasadena, Calif.

Relax Routine 11

(B) Right hand stays as in (A).

Place Left hand under tailbone, palm up or down, whichever is more comfortable.

TIME: 3 minutes

(C) Right hand stays as in (A).

Left hand holds below outer Right anklebone.

TIME: 3 minutes

REVERSE ROUTINE

This routine is as effective in lying position, if preferred.

NOTE: If several Self-Therap/Ease treatments, carefully selected and preceded by Relax Routine 1, do not relieve your condition, you should consult a physician.

head

Relieves simple frontal headaches...neck pains... discomforts of head colds.

Illustrated routine will help *LEFT* side.
To relieve *RIGHT* side, *REVERSE ROUTINE.*

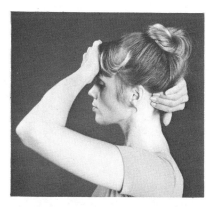

(A) Place Left hand across forehead, applying firm pressure
with palm and fingertips.

Right hand presses Left
base of head.

TIME: 3 minutes

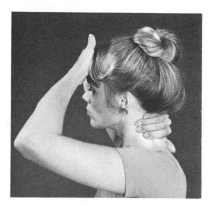

(B) Left hand stays as in (A).

Right hand holds Left side of
neck firmly.

TIME: 3 minutes

REVERSE ROUTINE

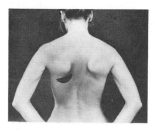

ADDED RELAXATION

This routine is as effective in lying
position, if preferred. For added relaxation,
place towel knot under Left lower shoulder
blade area. Reverse towel-knot position,
when routine is reversed.

50

sinus

Relieves discomforts of sinus, including related headaches.

Illustrated routine will help *BOTH* sides of head.

(A) Place thumbs on bones below eyebrows, close to bridge of nose, and press upward gently.

TIME: 3 minutes

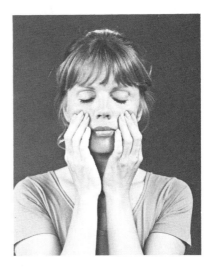

(B) Press gently upward under both cheekbones.

You may find this position more comfortable if you rest your elbows on a table.

TIME: 3 minutes

Important: Seated position helps loosened fluids drain more easily.

BEFORE SELECTING RELAX ROUTINE, *please read* "to feel better, sooner" *on page 161.*

sinus

Relieves stuffy nose. Alleviates sinus-caused eye problems, including twitching. Eases sinus pressure in head.

Illustrated routine will help *LEFT* side.
To relieve *RIGHT* side, *REVERSE ROUTINE.*

Important: Seated position helps loosened fluids drain more easily.

(A) Left hand presses Right upper shoulder blade area.

Right thumb presses gently upward under Left cheekbone as Right index finger holds Left forehead.

TIME: 3 minutes

(B) Left hand presses Right base of head.

Right hand presses gently upward under Left collarbone.

TIME: 3 minutes

REVERSE ROUTINE

sinus

Eases sinus congestion. Relaxes eye disorders related to sinus. Relieves post-nasal drip.

Illustrated routine will help *RIGHT* side.
To relieve *LEFT* side, *REVERSE ROUTINE.*

Right thumb presses inside corner of Right eye socket.

Left hand holds spine just above tailbone.

TIME: 3 minutes

ALWAYS REVERSE ROUTINE

Important: Seated position helps loosened fluids drain more easily.

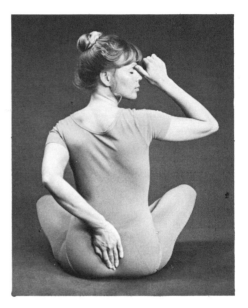

Sinus headaches seem to attack me for no reason. My head fills up. The pain is excruciating and I find it hard to breathe. The first time I used Self Therap/Ease it felt as though somebody had just put Drano down my head pipes. Best of all, the self-treatments really work!

NANCY DILLON (Clerk, Typist)
Panorama City, Calif.

Relax Routine 15

allergies

Relieves many discomforts of allergies.
Eases breathing. Reduces bloat in legs and ankles.

Illustrated routine will help *LEFT* side.
To relieve *RIGHT* side, *REVERSE ROUTINE.*

This routine is as effective
in lying position, if preferred.

(A) Right thumb presses Left
     inside upper arm.

     Cup Left fingers firmly around
     Left inner rib cage.

TIME: 3 minutes

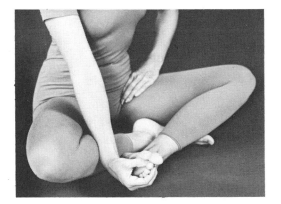

(B) Left hand presses into Left
     groin.

     Right thumb and index
     finger press Left toes firmly,
     one at a time, for one
     minute each.

TIME: 5 minutes

REVERSE ROUTINE

allergies

Eases hoarseness…dry cough.
Helps correct saliva problems.

Illustrated routine will help *ENTIRE* body.

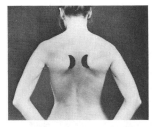

Lie on 2 towel knots
or sponge-rubber balls
on each side of spine,
in mid-shoulder blade area.

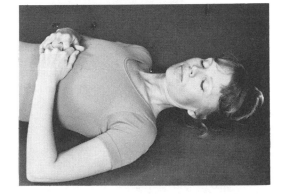

(A) Place comfortably-laced
fingers below breasts, so
that fingertips touch body.

TIME: 4 minutes

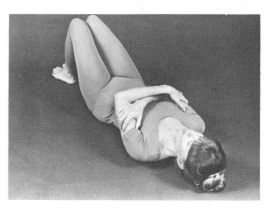

(B) Cross arms comfortably. Use
thumbs to press Right and
Left inside upper arms.

TIME: 4 minutes

If seated position is substituted,
added benefits of use of towel
knots would be lost.

ALWAYS USE BOTH HANDS (and towel knot or ball)
at **same time!** Self-Therap/Ease **combinations** speed relief.

allergies

Relieves stuffy head...dry throat...chest discomforts.

Illustrated routine will help *LEFT* side.
To relieve *RIGHT* side, *REVERSE ROUTINE.*

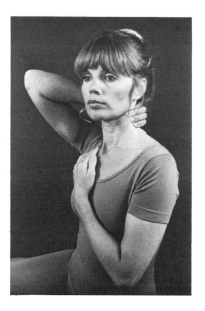

(A) Right hand holds Left side
of neck firmly.

Left hand presses gently
upward under
Right collarbone.

TIME: 3 minutes

I suffer from congestion caused by allergies (cigarette smoke, hay fever, pollen), and have had to use various medications. Since Betty Mehling told me how to do this simple routine, I have been able to cut down medications by 75%.

LEAH RADSTONE (College Student)
Westwood, Calif.

Relax Routine 18

allergies

(B) Right hand stays as in (A).

Left hand presses Right
inner rib cage.

TIME: 3 minutes

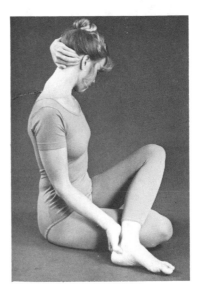

(C) Right thumb presses
below inner Left anklebone.

Left hand presses bone
behind Right ear.

TIME: 3 minutes

REVERSE ROUTINE

This routine is as effective
in lying position, if preferred.

stomach

Eases most chronic stomach problems...dry mouth ...chapped lips. Relieves swollen knees and top-of-thigh discomforts. Alleviates related depression.

Illustrated routine will help *LEFT* side.
To relieve *RIGHT* side, *REVERSE ROUTINE.*

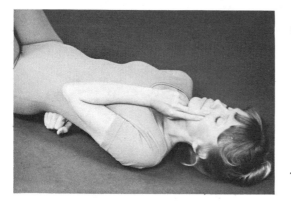

(A) Left hand presses under Left cheekbone, close to nose.

Place Right fist under Left waist. In seated position, leaning back into fist increases effectiveness of this step.

TIME: 3 minutes

Two years ago, I had extensive surgery to remove an abscess on my colon. Although the surgery was successful, I still get "gassy" feelings, which antacid-type medications do not relieve. I now use this self-help, recommended by Betty Mehling, and find that it relieves the pressure and pain in that area.

SUZI SPECTOR (Student)
Sherman Oaks, Calif.

Relax Routine 19

TIME RECOMMENDED for each step in Routines is minimum. Devote **as much time** as you find helpful. Self-Therap/Ease can not harm you.

(B) Left hand stays as in (A).

    Right hand presses top of Left thigh.

TIME: 3 minutes

(C) Left hand holds outside of Left shinbone, about 4 inches below knee.

    Right fist returns to Left waist, as in (A).

TIME: 3 minutes

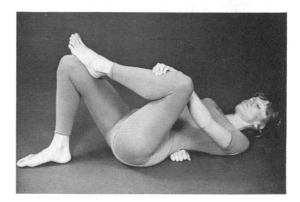

REVERSE ROUTINE

This routine is as effective in seated position, if preferred.

KEEP IN MIND that **Self**-Therap/Ease is a **supplementary** therapy — **not** a substitute for attention by a physician, or a qualified practitioner of Therap/Ease.

stomach

Relieves minor stomach pains…intestinal gas.
Loosens chest congestion.

Illustrated routine will help *ENTIRE* body.

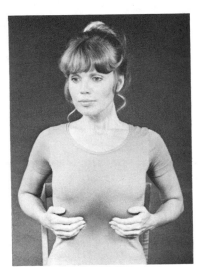

(A) Cup fingers of both hands firmly around both sides of inner rib cage.

TIME: 3 minutes

Bonnie Pendleton taught me a simple routine to help myself. Within five minutes I can relax and revive my energy level… by putting my fists upright on either side of my spine above the waist. It's as if somebody gave me a magic formula. I always begin with Relax Routine 1.

SAUREET HAYILL (Writer/Editor)
Los Angeles, Calif.

See "for openers", page 33, and Relax Routine 1

stomach

(B) Press both hands firmly into
Left and Right groin
at same time.

TIME: 3 minutes

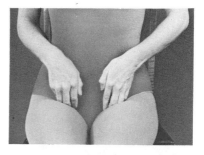

(C) Cross hands. Place fists at
inner thighs, about 3 inches
above knees. Press legs into
your fists as hard as you can.
You may find this step more
comfortable lying,
on either side.

TIME: 3 minutes

This routine is as effective
in lying position, if preferred.

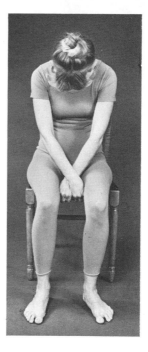

---

please remember....
RELAX ROUTINE 1 IS ALSO **"for openers."**
While you will find this Routine an excellent
9-minute over-all Relaxer at any time — this
procedure is especially beneficial to begin helping
your self with SELF-THERAP/EASE.

stomach

Relieves minor stomach distress.

Illustrated routine will help *ENTIRE* body.

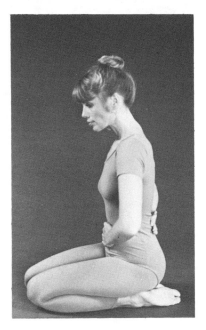

Place Right hand on your back,
behind discomfort.

Place Left hand firmly
on discomfort.

TIME: 3 minutes

REPEAT 3 times; every
10 minutes for one-half hour
until pain subsides.

This routine is as effective
in lying position, if desired.

---

*As a theatrical agent, I am often away from home for a week
at a time. On one of these trips, I suddenly developed a
pounding toothache. Remembering the simple Relax Routines I learned, I managed to control the pain for all week-
end, until I could get home to my dentist. Thank heaven for
Self-Therap/Ease!*

EARLENE SMITH (Theatrical Agent)
Los Angeles, Calif.

Relax Routines 33 and 50

nausea

Relieves symptoms of vomiting caused by stomach upsets, if applied at first warning.

It is important that you follow *BOTH* the Routine illustrated
AND the *REVERSE ROUTINE* at end of this procedure.

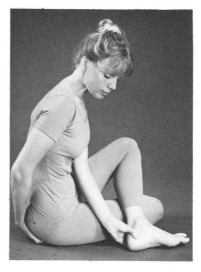

This routine is as effective
in lying position, if preferred.

(A) Place Right hand under
tailbone, palm up or down,
whichever is more comfortable.

Left thumb presses below
inner Left anklebone.

TIME: 3 minutes

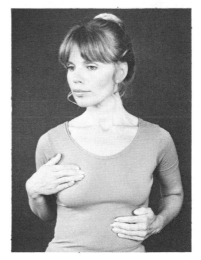

(B) Place Right hand gently on
Right upper breast.

Cup Left fingers firmly around
Left inner rib cage.

TIME: 3 minutes

ALWAYS REVERSE ROUTINE

CAUTION: Do NOT use lying position
if there is danger of vomiting. This may
cause choking. If there is indication
of appendicitis, call your doctor.

nausea

Relieves feelings of nausea....
pressure in abdominal area.

It is important that you follow *BOTH* the Routine illustrated
AND the *REVERSE ROUTINE* at end of this procedure.

Right index and middle fingers
press gently upward under Right
cheekbone, close to nose.

Left thumb and index finger press
Right big toe firmly.

TIME: 3 minutes

ALWAYS REVERSE ROUTINE

This routine is as effective
in lying position, if preferred.

CAUTION: Do NOT use lying position
if there is danger of vomiting. This may
cause choking. If there is indication
of appendicitis, call your doctor.

*One day, while visiting Betty Mehling, a sudden wave of
nausea came over me. She told me; "Sit down, put your
fingers under your cheekbone close to your nose, and hold
your big toe — same side." I did. Within a couple of minutes
the pressure disappeared and I felt great!*
WENDY STEINMETZ (Grade School Teacher)
Woodland Hills, California

Relax Routine 23

nausea

Relieves nauseous feeling in lower intestine.

Illustrated routine will help *ENTIRE* body.

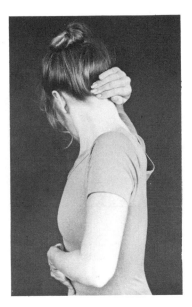

Right hand presses Center base of head.

Place Left index finger in navel. Gently lift finger slightly upward (toward head) and hold.

TIME: 3 minutes

This Relax Routine is more effective when applied in reclining position.

PLEASE SEE NOTE ON FACING PAGE.

Between being a student, keeping our 5-year-old son busy, and helping my husband as his "girl Friday", I must feel great all the time. Besides those activities, I'm pregnant again. I have no time for nausea, fatigue, bloat or backaches. Betty has given me several Self-Therap/Ease routines that take a very short time, and really work well for me. This Routine rid me of "morning" sickness.

                        NANCI GAMACHE (Homemaker/Student)

                                 Calabasas, Calif.

Relax Routine 24

indigestion

Relieves abdominal discomforts and chest congestion.

Illustrated routine will help *ENTIRE* body.

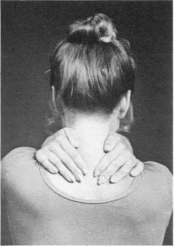

Illustrated to show position of hands.

(A) Press both Right and Left
upper shoulder blade areas.
Cross arms if
more comfortable.

TIME: 3 minutes

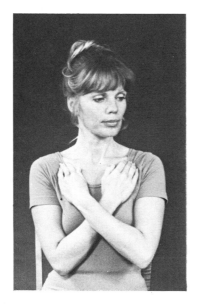

(B) Cross arms and press fingertips gently upward under both
sides of collarbone.

TIME: 3 minutes

NOTE: If several Self-Therap/Ease treatments, carefully selected and preceded by
Relax Routine 1, do not relieve your condition, you are urged to consult a physician.

indigestion

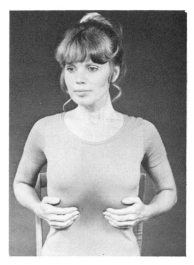

(C) Cup fingers of both hands firmly around both sides of inner rib cage.

TIME: 3 minutes

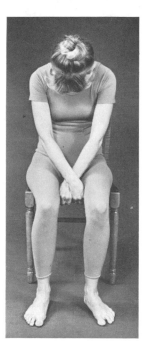

(D) Cross hands. Place fists at inner thighs, about 3 inches above knees. Press legs into your fists as hard as you can. You may find this step more comfortable lying, *on either side.*

TIME: 3 minutes

This routine is as effective in lying position, if preferred.

indigestion

Relieves simple indigestion.
Eases side-of-neck and shoulder tensions.

Illustrated routine will help *RIGHT* side.
To relieve *LEFT* side, *REVERSE ROUTINE.*

Left hand presses Right upper
shoulder blade area.

Right thumb presses gently
upward under Left cheekbone as
Right index finger holds
Left forehead.

TIME: 3 minutes

REVERSE ROUTINE

This routine is as effective
in lying position, if preferred.

*Self-Therap/Ease Routines are the only natural ways I have
found to help myself soothe stomach problems. These easy
self-treatments are such comforts. I get relief so simply.
Thanks to Self-Therap/Ease, no more sleepless nights, no
more indigestion.*

PAT WHITEMAN (Homemaker)

Canyon Country, Calif.

Relax Routine 26

bloat

Reduces facial bloat...bags under eyes... complexion problems.

Illustrated routine will help *ENTIRE* face.

Place towel knot. under tailbone.

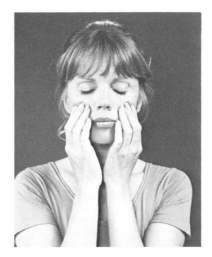

(A) Press gently upward under both cheekbones.

You may find this position more comfortable if you rest your elbows on a table.

TIME: 3 minutes

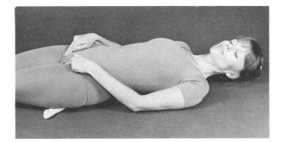

(B) Press hands firmly into Left and Right groin at same time.

TIME: 3 minutes

This routine is equally effective in either lying or seated position.

69

bloat

Reduces general bloat...dizziness.
Relieves lower back and tailbone pains...
simple kidney discomforts.

Illustrated routine will help *RIGHT* side.
To relieve *LEFT* side, *REVERSE ROUTINE.*

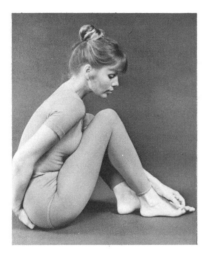

(A) Place Right hand under tailbone, palm up or down, whichever is more comfortable.

Left thumb and index finger
hold Right little toe firmly.

TIME: 3 minutes

*I have found that these self-procedures not only heighten
effectiveness of Therap/Ease with which Betty Mehling has
helped me for years. Self-Therap/Ease relieves chronic low
backaches. These self-treatments have also cleared my complexion, removed dark circles under my eyes...and have even
stopped my hiccups.*

WENDY FISHER (Management Analyst)
Westlake Village, Calif.

Relax Routine 28

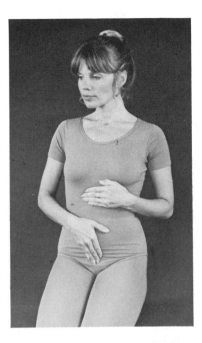

(B) Right hand presses pubic bone.

Left hand presses Right inner
rib cage.

TIME: 3 minutes

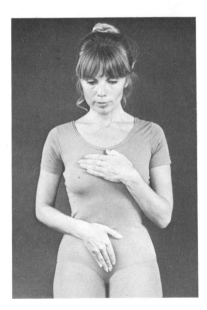

(C) Right hand stays as in (B).

Place Left hand gently
on Right upper breast.

TIME: 3 minutes

REVERSE ROUTINE

This routine is as effective
in lying position, if preferred.

bloat

Relieves general body water retention.
Eases discomforts in knees and ankles.

Illustrated routine will help *LEFT* side.
To relieve *RIGHT* side, *REVERSE ROUTINE.*

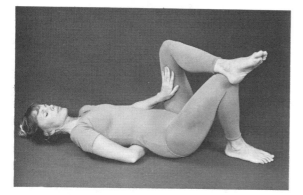

(A) Place Right fist under Left waist. In seated position, leaning back into fist increases effectiveness.

Left hand presses Left inner thigh.

TIME: 3 minutes

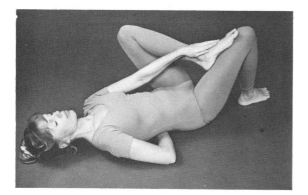

(B) Right fist stays as in (A).

Left hand holds top of Left foot.

TIME: 3 minutes

REVERSE ROUTINE

This routine is as effective in seated position, if preferred.

bloat

Relieves stomach bloat and gas in lower digestive tract.

Illustrated routine will help *ENTIRE* body.

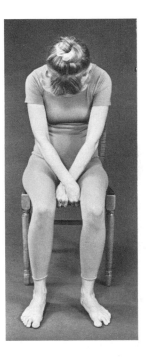

Cross hands. Place fists at inner thighs, about 3 inches above knees. Press legs into your fists as hard as you can. You may find this step more comfortable lying, *on either side.*

TIME: 3 minutes
(or longer if you wish)

Since I was a young girl, indigestion had always plagued me — until I found Self-Therap/Ease. This is such an easy way to relieve bloat and stomach distress. Hardly a night goes by that I don't use this Relax Routine and feel much better for it. I am now 74.

WYNN HOFFINE (Homemaker)
Glendale, Calif.

Relax Routine 30

neck

Relieves side-of-neck pains.
Eases discomforts in elbows and hands.

Illustrated routine will help *LEFT* side.
To relieve *RIGHT* side, *REVERSE ROUTINE.*

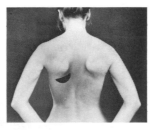

Place towel knot under Left
lower shoulder blade area.

If seated position is substituted,
added benefits of use of towel
knot would be lost.

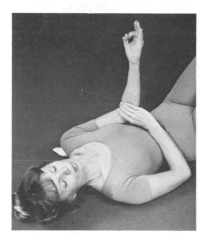

(A) Right hand holds
   Left inner elbow.

   Left thumb presses
   Left fingernails, one at a time,
   for one minute each.

TIME: 4 minutes

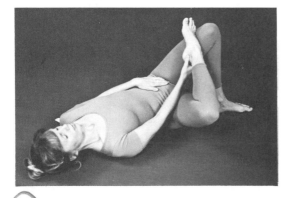

(B) Right thumb presses below
   inner Right anklebone.

   Left hand presses into
   Left groin.

TIME: 3 minutes

**REVERSE ROUTINE AND
TOWEL-KNOT POSITION.**

74

neck

Relieves neck stiffness... pains in shoulder blades...mid-back aches.

Illustrated routine will help *LEFT* side.
To relieve *RIGHT* side, *REVERSE ROUTINE.*

Place towel knot under Left lower shoulder blade area.

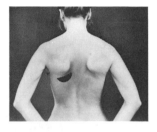

Place Left fist under Left waist.

Right hand holds Left side of neck firmly.

TIME: 4 minutes

REVERSE ROUTINE AND TOWEL-KNOT POSITION.

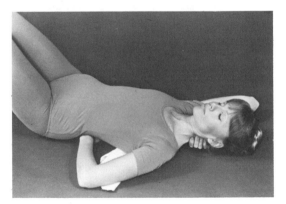

My doctor referred me to Bonnie Pendleton. The simple exercises she gave me to do at home took the tensions out of my neck and shoulders. This self-treatment worked so well for me that now my husband also uses Self-Therap/Ease. It is a great way to start and end the day.

CAND. I HUBERT (Store Manager)
North Hollywood, Calif.

Relax Routine 32

75

neck

Eases chronic stiff neck. Reduces intestinal bloat. Relieves throat discomforts.

Illustrated routine will help *RIGHT* side.
To relieve *LEFT* side, *REVERSE ROUTINE.*

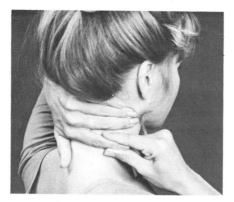

This routine is equally effective in either lying or seated position.

(A) Left hand holds Right side of neck firmly.

Right thumb and index finger firmly hold Left index finger.

TIME: 3 minutes

As a Therap/Ease practitioner, I constantly work with my arms and hands. After hours of these efforts, my neck and shoulders are often tense. Before going to bed, I use this relaxing Self-Therap/Ease Routine. My tensions are soon relieved. Those I help likewise find relief in the Therap/Ease self-treatments I suggest. These routines soothe them and make my work easier.

FRANCES SPRATT (Practitioner of Therap/Ease)
Glendale, Calif.

Relax Routine 33

(B) Left hand stays as in (A).

Place Right hand gently on Right upper breast.

TIME: 3 minutes

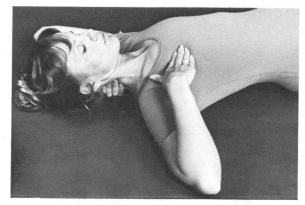

(C) Left hand stays as in (A).

Right thumb presses gently upward under Left cheekbone, close to nose.

TIME: 3 minutes

REVERSE ROUTINE

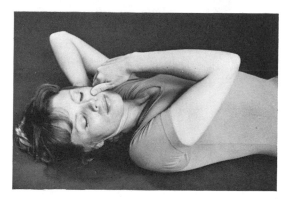

MAINTAIN FIRM PRESSURE. For the first few self-treatments, accumulated tensions will likely make affected areas tender to hold. Regular use of Relax Routines will remove the sensitivity, and eliminate causes of tension tenderness — at the source.

neck

Relieves neck discomfort...shoulder pain.

Illustrated routine will help *LEFT* side.
To relieve *RIGHT* side, *REVERSE ROUTINE.*

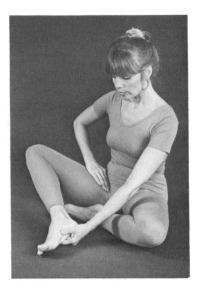

(A) Right hand presses into
Right groin.

Left thumb presses outer
edge of Right arch.

TIME: 3 minutes

After finding relief for long-term low back problems through Therap/Ease, I wondered how I could help rid myself of neck/shoulder pains. Betty Mehling recommended this simple exercise. I was delighted with how quickly it helped me lose my discomforts. As a paramedic, I have learned how to help others in times of emergency. Through Self-Therap/Ease, I have learned how to help myself naturally.

RON D'ACCHIOLI (Paramedic)

Burbank, Calif.

Relax Routine 34

(B) Right hand stays as in (A).

   Left hand presses Right upper
   shoulder blade area.

TIME: 3 minutes

(C) Right hand holds Left side of
   neck firmly.

   Left thumb presses gently
   upward under Right cheekbone as Left index finger holds
   Right forehead.

TIME: 3 minutes

REVERSE ROUTINE

This routine is as effective
in lying position, if preferred.

arms

Relieves sore arm muscles.

Illustrated routine will help *LEFT* side.
To relieve *RIGHT* side, *REVERSE ROUTINE.*

Right hand presses middle of
Left shoulder blade.

Left hand presses top of Left foot,
about 2 inches above base of toes.

TIME: 4 minutes

REVERSE ROUTINE

This routine is as effective
in lying position, if preferred.

*Calligraphy is an exacting and tedious craft. After working
for a while, my arms and hands get tense. By stopping long
enough to do this simple exercise Bonnie showed me, I get
quick relief. Then my work goes faster and easier. This is
only one of several Self-Therap/Ease Relax Routines I find
helpful every day.*

J. D. ABBOTT (Artist/Calligrapher)
Tarzana, Calif.

Relax Routine 35

arms

Relieves shoulder pains. Eases problems in extending arms. Relaxes finger tensions.

Illustrated routine will help LEFT side.
To relieve RIGHT side, REVERSE ROUTINE.

Place towel knot under Left outer shoulder blade area.

If seated position is substituted, added benefits of use of towel knot would be lost.

(A) Right hand holds Left inner elbow.

Left hand presses Right upper shoulder blade area.

TIME: 3 minutes

(B) Right thumb and index finger firmly hold Left fingers, below knuckle, one at a time, for one minute each.

TIME: 5 minutes

REVERSE ROUTINE

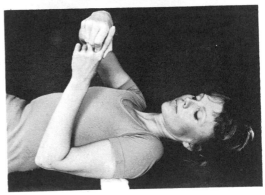

81

arms

Relieves upper arm and elbow pains... damp palms...chest discomfort.

Illustrated routine will help RIGHT side.
To relieve LEFT side, REVERSE ROUTINE.

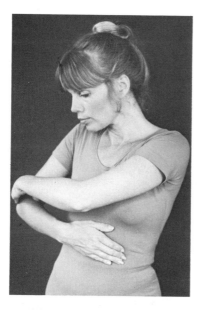

(A) Left thumb holds Right inner elbow.

Right hand presses into Left inner rib cage.

TIME: 3 minutes

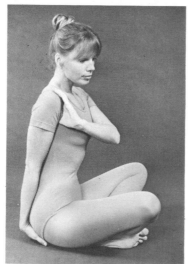

(B) Left thumb presses into Right armpit.

Place Right hand under Right buttock.

TIME: 3 minutes

REVERSE ROUTINE

This routine is as effective in lying position, if preferred.

arms

Relieves arm/neck/back tensions. Eases elbow discomforts, including "tennis elbow".

*Illustrated routine will help RIGHT side.
To relieve LEFT side, REVERSE ROUTINE.*

Place towel knot under Right lower shoulder blade area.

If seated position is substituted, added benefits of use of towel knot would be lost.

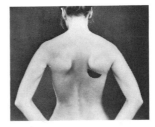

(A) Right hand presses Right upper shoulder blade area.

Left hand holds Right outer shoulder blade area.

TIME: 3 minutes

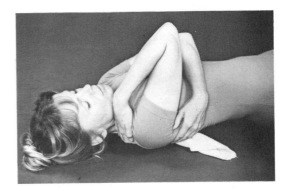

(B) Right hand stays as in (A).

Left hand presses into Right groin.

TIME: 3 minutes

REVERSE ROUTINE AND TOWEL-KNOT POSITION.

legs

Relieves most leg pains...discomforts of varicose veins. Reduces general bloat. Eases tightness in shoulder blades.

Illustrated routine will help *RIGHT* side.
To relieve *LEFT* side, *REVERSE ROUTINE.*

(A) Place Right hand under Right buttock.

Left hand presses middle of Right shoulder blade.

TIME: 3 minutes

Every day I get more proof from those I help that Therap/ Ease is the simplest and best form of Asiatic healing by hand. This proof comes not only from clients and friends who use the self-helps I suggest. Thanks to Self-Therap/ Ease I feel 20 years younger. Now, with this long-awaited book of authentic Oriental self-therapy, many more people will be helping themselves to better health.

RUTH WONG (Practitioner of Therap/Ease)
Sunland, Calif.

Relax Routine 39

(B) Right hand stays as in (A).

    Left hand holds outside upper
    Right calf.

TIME: 3 minutes

(C) Right hand stays as in (A).

    Left hand holds top of
    Right foot.

TIME: 3 minutes

REVERSE ROUTINE

This routine is as effective
in lying position, if preferred.

AND REMEMBER, EVERY BODY IS DIFFERENT.
Allow for variations when you select Routines!

legs

**Relieves foot and leg tensions…ankle discomforts.
Eases lower back pains.
Reduces difficulties in urinating.**

Illustrated routine will help *ENTIRE* body.

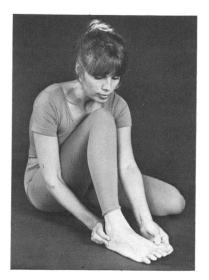

(A) Right hand holds below both
sides of Right anklebone: with
thumb below inner bone, index
and middle fingers below
outer bone.

Left thumb and index finger
firmly hold Right toes, one at
a time, for one minute each.

TIME: 5 minutes

(B) Repeat (A) on Left foot.

TIME: 5 minutes

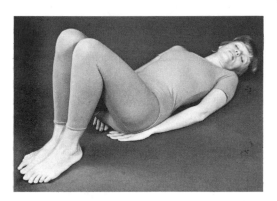

(C) Lie on hands, palms down,
under back of hips.

TIME: 3 minutes

legs

Eases leg pains and fatigue.

Illustrated routine will help *LEFT* side.
To relieve *RIGHT* side, *REVERSE ROUTINE.*

Place Left hand under Left
buttock, palm up or down,
whichever is more comfortable.

Right hand holds under
Left knee.

TIME: 4 minutes

REVERSE ROUTINE

This routine is as effective sitting in a
chair or in lying position, as preferred.

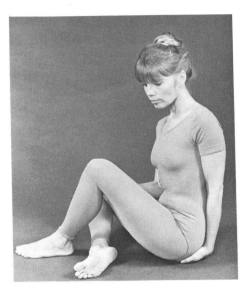

*After a summer of loafing, I returned to school to find cheer-
leading practice was scheduled daily. After the first couple
of days, my legs ached so much that I could hardly walk.
Betty Mehling, who had helped a neighbor of ours, suggested
this easy exercise. I felt relief within minutes! Cheers for Self-
Therap/Ease!*

CONNIE GRANTHAM (High School Senior)
Calabasas, Calif.

Relax Routine 41

legs

Relaxes outer ankle and toe tensions. Relieves outer calves and thigh pains. Eases hip discomforts.

Illustrated routine will help *LEFT* side.
To relieve *RIGHT* side, *REVERSE ROUTINE.*

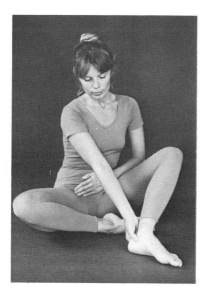

(A) Right thumb presses below inner Left anklebone.

Left hand presses into Right groin.

TIME: 3 minutes

At last, the easy Relax Routines used by my family for years are in book form. The leg and hip problems which have been with me most of my life have been relieved by my turning on my own Power Centers. As I tell my friends, it's all in knowing your own combinations.

RITA DI GIOVANNI (Bookkeeper)
Mission Hills, Calif.

Relax Routine 42

(B) Right hand stays as in (A).

Left thumb and index finger
firmly hold Left toes,
one at a time, for
one minute each.

TIME: 5 minutes

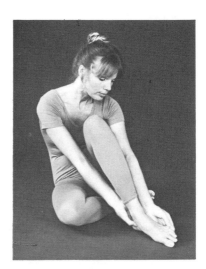

(C) Always lie on back for (C).
Right hand holds outside
upper Left calf.

Place Left hand under
back of Left hip.

TIME: 3 minutes

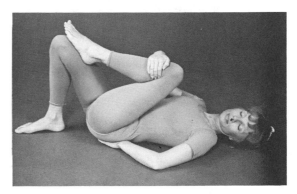

REVERSE ROUTINE

This routine is as effective if (A) and (B)
are also done in lying-down position.

feet

Relieves fatigue and pains in feet and legs.
Relaxes lower back and buttocks.

Illustrated routine will help *LEFT* side.
To relieve *RIGHT* side, *REVERSE ROUTINE.*

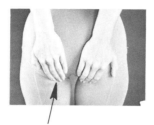

Place towel knot
under Left buttock.

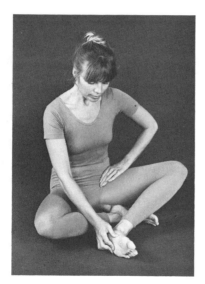

(A) Left hand presses into
Left groin.

Right thumb presses outer
edge of Left arch.

TIME: 3 minutes

KEEP IN MIND that **Self**-Therap/Ease is a **supplementary** therapy — **not** a substitute for attention by a physician, or a qualified practitioner of Therap/Ease.

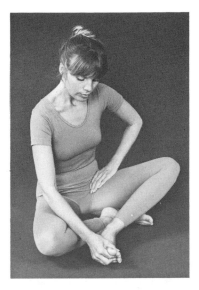

(B) Left hand stays as in (A).

Right thumb and index finger
firmly hold Left toes, one at a
time, for one minute each.

TIME: 5 minutes

(C) Left hand stays as in (A).

Right hand holds outside
upper Left calf.

TIME: 3 minutes

REVERSE ROUTINE

This routine is as effective
in lying position, if preferred.

feet

Eases discomforts of corns, calluses and bunions.

Illustrated routine will help *RIGHT* side.
To relieve *LEFT* side, *REVERSE ROUTINE.*

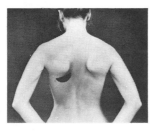

Causes of corns, calluses and bunions may
be improperly fitted shoes or hosiery,
or other conditions which require attention
of a podiatrist.

Place towel knot under Left
lower shoulder blade area.

(A) Right hand presses pubic bone.

Left thumb holds outer edge of
Right arch.

TIME: 3 minutes

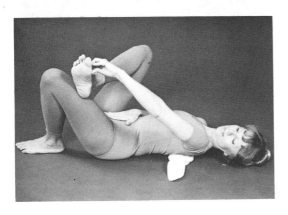

(B) Right hand stays as in (A).

Left hand holds bunion, corn
or callus on Right foot.

TIME: 3 minutes

**REVERSE ROUTINE AND
TOWEL-KNOT POSITION.**

Repeat twice daily until
condition is eased.

arthritis

Relieves arthritic pains in legs, and other parts of the body. Eases leg fatigue.

Illustrated routine will help *RIGHT* side.
To relieve *LEFT* side, *REVERSE ROUTINE.*

Place Right hand under
Right buttock.

Left hand holds behind Right
anklebone (both sides) firmly.

TIME: 3 minutes

REVERSE ROUTINE

This routine is as effective
in lying position, if preferred.

A series of self-treatments, instructed by Bonnie Pendleton, not only relieved my severe pains of arthritis — they continue to help set right almost everything else in my body that needs help.

VIRGINIA HENDERSON (Retiree)
Westwood, Calif.

Relax Routine 45

arthritis

Relieves arthritic pains, and fatigue in legs and feet...gout.

Illustrated routine will help *ENTIRE* body.

Place towel knot
under tailbone.

This routine is equally effective
in either lying or seated position.

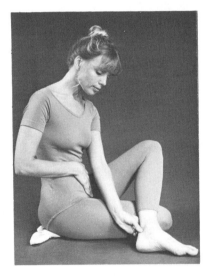

(A) Right hand presses pubic bone.

Left hand holds behind Left
anklebone (both sides) firmly.

TIME: 3 minutes

(B) REVERSE (A)

TIME: 3 minutes

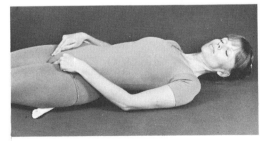

(C) Press hands firmly into
Left and Right groin at
same time.

TIME: 3 minutes

ALWAYS USE BOTH HANDS (and towel knot or ball)
at **same time!** Self-Therap/Ease **combinations** speed relief.

arthritis

Eases arthritic pains or fatigue in arms and hands.

Illustrated routine will help *LEFT* side.
To relieve *RIGHT* side, *REVERSE ROUTINE.*

Place towel knot under Left
lower shoulder blade area.

If seated position is substituted,
added benefits of use of towel
knot would be lost.

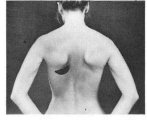

(A) Right thumb and index finger
firmly hold Left fingers, below
knuckle, one at a time, for one
minute each.

TIME: 5 minutes

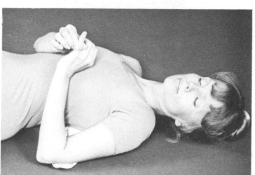

(B) Right hand holds Left
inner elbow.

TIME: 3 minutes

**REVERSE ROUTINE AND
TOWEL-KNOT POSITION.**

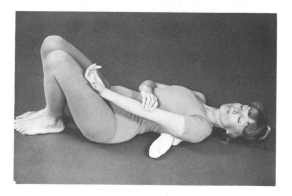

IF YOU NEED RELIEF on the same side (Left or Right), as
illustrated in Relax Routine, go ahead! Should your problem
be on the **other** side, REVERSE ROUTINE, as on page 26.

fractures

Helps heal broken leg, ankle and toe bones. Relieves tensions, sprains, fatigue in legs, ankles and toes.

Illustrated routine will help *LEFT* side.
To relieve *RIGHT* side, *REVERSE ROUTINE.*

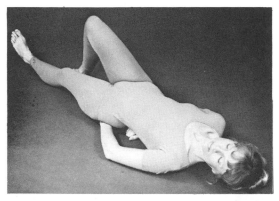

(A) Place Right fist under Left waist. In seated position, leaning back into fist increases effectiveness.

Place Left fist (preferred) — or flat of Left hand — at back of Left hip area.

TIME: 3 minutes

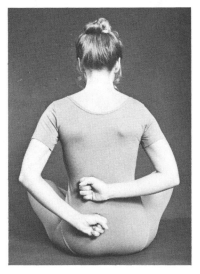

BACK VIEW

Illustrated to show positions of hands.

(B) Right fist stays as in (A).

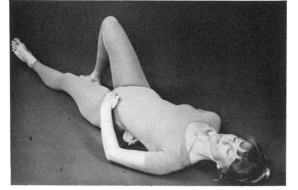

    Left hand presses
    into Left groin.

TIME: 3 minutes

REVERSE ROUTINE

NOTE: Relax Routines 48 and 49 are intended
only as therapies to help speed healing of
fractured bones, which have been set by
orthopedist. In some cases, healing processes
are slowed by dietary deficiencies or other
causes, which should be treated by orthopedic
surgeon or physician.

FISTSFUL OF RELIEF!

*If Relax Routine calls for your hands behind your back —
whether you are lying down or seated — you will get relief
more quickly by using your doubled-up fists, rather than
the flats of your hands. Fists are especially effective when
self-treatments include inner-thigh position. Any tenderness
you may feel from this procedure will gradually diminish as
the congestion causing the sensitivity is corrected through
Self-Therap/Ease. In places awkward or uncomfortable for
fists to reach, towel knot or rubber ball (explained on page
25) may be preferred.*

fractures

Helps heal broken arm, wrist and finger bones. Relieves tensions, sprains, fatigue in arms, wrists and fingers.

Illustrated routine will help *LEFT* side.
To relieve *RIGHT* side, *REVERSE ROUTINE.*

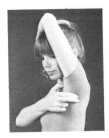

Place towel knot under Left outer shoulder blade area.

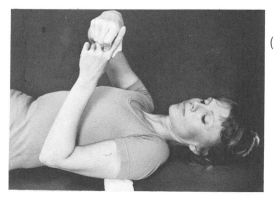

(A) Right hand presses into Left groin.

TIME: 3 minutes

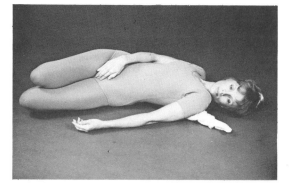

(B) Right thumb and index finge[r] firmly hold Left fingers, belo[w] knuckle, one at a time, for o[ne] minute each.

TIME: 5 minutes

REVERSE ROUTINE AN[D] TOWEL-KNOT POSITION

teeth

Reduces pains of simple toothaches.

Illustrated routine helps relieve toothaches on *RIGHT* side.
To relieve toothaches on *LEFT* side, follow *REVERSE ROUTINE.*

NOTE: This routine is not intended for conditions such as abscess or infection. If this Routine, repeated often, does not relieve discomfort, you are urged to consult your dentist.

UPPER TOOTHACHES

Right hand holds pain area.

Spread Left fingers across upper arm, halfway between elbow and shoulder.

TIME: 4 minutes

REVERSE ROUTINE FOR UPPER TOOTHACHES ON LEFT SIDE.

LOWER TOOTHACHES

Right hand holds pain area.

Spread Left fingers across outside leg area, halfway between knee and anklebone.

TIME: 4 minutes

REVERSE ROUTINE FOR LOWER TOOTHACHES ON LEFT SIDE.

Repeat as often as needed until discomfort is eased.

99

insomnia

Induces natural sleep. Alleviates ringing in ears. Relaxes menstrual cramps.

Illustrated routine will help *LEFT* side.
To relieve *RIGHT* side, *REVERSE ROUTINE.*

(A) Right hand presses bone behind Left ear.

Left hand holds Left side of forehead.

TIME: 3 minutes

This routine is as effective in seated position, if preferred.

reminder...

SELF-THERAP/EASE is a **preventive** as well as **corrective** healing art. Self-treatments designed to relieve and control bothersome conditions should be continued **regularly.** Severe problems often require two or three repeats of Relax Routines daily until eased. After that, or in cases of mild discomforts, Self-Therap/Ease once a day will bring continued relaxation and relief of common pains.

(B) Right hand stays as in (A).

    Cup Left fingers firmly around
    Left inner rib cage.

TIME: 3 minutes

(C) Right hand stays as in (A).

    Place Left hand under Left
    buttock, palm up or down,
    whichever is more
    comfortable.

TIME: 3 minutes

REVERSE ROUTINE

Illustrated to show positions of hands.

FOR BEST OVER-ALL RESULTS, *always* Reverse procedure, if so instructed at the end of Routine. Even though you seem to be more uncomfortable on *one* side, correcting imbalances or obstructions on *both* sides will speed the chain reaction Nature intended to help your *entire* body.

insomnia

Relaxes body to normal sleep.
Illustrated routine will help *ENTIRE* body.

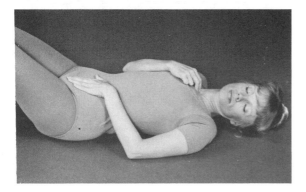

Place Right hand gently on depression in front of neck.

Left hand presses pubic bone.

TIME: 4 minutes

Because of my work, I am keyed-up much of the time. Trying to turn off my mind at the end of the day so that I could sleep used to be a problem for me. These Routines I learned both work well on me. Often when I get into bed, my thoughts may still be reeling from the day's activities. Several minutes after I finish either of these routines, complete relaxation takes over my entire body and mind. Almost before I know just what is happening, I fall asleep, and enjoy a full night's natural sleep.

ANNE WALKER (Advertising)
Sacramento, California

Relax Routines 52 and 53

insomnia

Relaxes mind and body, inducing sleep.

Illustrated routine will help *ENTIRE* body.

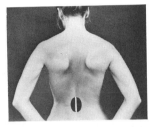

Lie on 2 towel knots,
or sponge-rubber balls,
one on each side of spine,
under waist.

(A) Lie on laced fingers, with
thumbs pressing on Left and
Right bases of skull.

TIME: 3 minutes

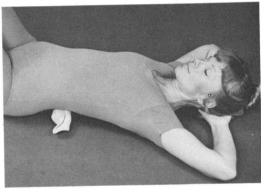

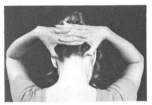

BACK VIEW

(B) Cup fingers of both hands
firmly around both sides of
inner rib cage.

TIME: 3 minutes

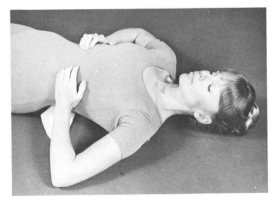

dizziness

Relieves occasional dizzy feelings. Eases eyestrain... neck pains...discomforts of nausea.

Illustrated routine will help *LEFT* side.
To relieve *RIGHT* side, *REVERSE ROUTINE.*

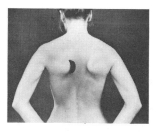

While this routine may be followed in seated position, effectiveness of use of towel knot would be lost.

Place towel knot under Left mid-shoulder blade area.

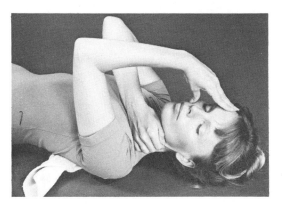

(A) Right hand holds Left side of neck firmly.

Left thumb presses gently upward under Right cheekbone as Left index finger holds Right forehead.

TIME: 3 minutes

Car accidents — all either directly or indirectly involving whiplashes — have left me with many neck tensions. I found much relief from Therap/Ease by Betty Mehling. But since my neck is a weak area, and my work involves much driving and mental pressure, tension keeps building up there. The Self-Therap/Ease Betty has taught me relieves the pains. Regular use of these self-routines reduces my need for her help. I find that this Relax Routine helps me very much.

MANNY JACOBS (Salesman)
Calabasas, Calif.

Relax Routine 54

dizziness

(B) Right hand stays as in (A).

Left thumb presses inside upper Right arm.

TIME: 3 minutes

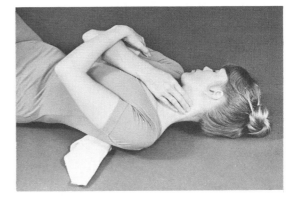

(C) Right hand stays as in (A).

Left hand gently presses base of breastbone (sternum).

TIME: 3 minutes

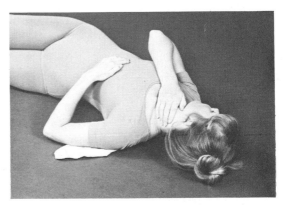

REVERSE ROUTINE AND TOWEL-KNOT POSITION.

NOTE: If dizzy when lying flat, elevate head with pillow.

please remember....
*RELAX ROUTINE 1 IS ALSO **"for openers."***
While you will find this Routine an excellent 9-minute over-all Relaxer at any time — this procedure is especially beneficial to begin helping your self with SELF-THERAP/EASE.

dizziness

Clears simple dizziness. Relaxes tensions at base of head. Relieves sinus and head discomforts. Eases minor backaches.

Illustrated routine will help *ENTIRE* body.

Place towel knot under tailbone.

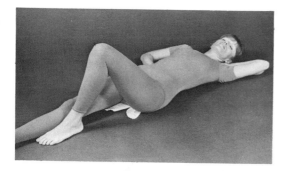

(A) Place Right fist under spine at waist. In seated position, leaning back into fist increases effectiveness.

Left hand holds spine in line with upper shoulder blade areas.

TIME: 3 minutes

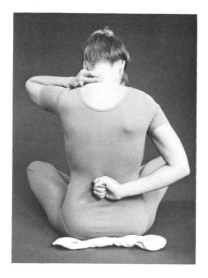

BACK VIEW
Illustrated to show positions of hands.

NOTE: If dizzy when lying flat, elevate head with pillow.

dizziness

(B) Right thumb presses between eyes gently.

Left hand presses pubic bone.

TIME: 3 minutes

This routine is as effective
in seated position, if preferred.

Listening to people's problems day after day began to reflect in both my feelings and my appearance. Using Self-Therap/ Ease daily has relieved both my physical and mental tensions. I feel great, I look younger and I urge my clients and other troubled people to use any of these self-treatments as I do.

BILL YOUNG (Psychologist)
Sunland, Calif.

Relax Routine 55

reminder...

WHEN should Relax Routines be used? Whether your problem is of long duration, or you've just begun to feel it — start Self-Therap/Ease **at once!** The sooner you start, the sooner you'll feel results! And the less chance of the tension or ache developing into a serious situation.

ears

Eases common earaches...tensions at base of head.
Reduces facial bloat.

Illustrated routine will help *RIGHT* side of head.
To relieve *LEFT* side of head, follow *REVERSE ROUTINE.*

(A) Place Right fist under Right waist. In seated position, leaning back into fist increases effectiveness .

Left hand presses bone behind Right ear.

TIME: 3 minutes

Please see *NOTE* on page 110.

While on vacation, I did a lot of diving and developed a bad ear infection. I was examined by a doctor and took medication, but I still felt pressure in my ear. By using this simple routine, in conjunction with my doctor's advice, the remaining pressure/pain was relieved. My complete recovery was speeded up.

RON BRYCHTA (Firefighter)
Sun Valley, Calif.

Relax Routine 56

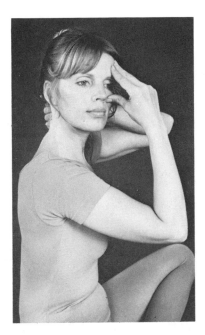

(B) Right thumb presses gently
    upward under Left cheekbone
    as Right index finger holds
    Left forehead.

Left hand presses
Right base of skull.

TIME: 3 minutes

Left hand position.

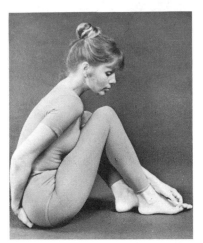

(C) Place Right hand under tail-
    bone, palm up or down,
    whichever is more comfortable.

Left thumb and index finger
firmly hold Right small toe.

TIME: 3 minutes

REVERSE ROUTINE

This routine is as effective
in lying position, if preferred.

ears

Relieves simple earaches...tensions behind eyes...sinus discomforts.

Illustrated routine will help *LEFT* side of head.
To relieve *RIGHT* side of head, follow *REVERSE ROUTINE.*

NOTE: Ears are complex mechanisms. If Routines illustrated here and on preceding pages do not relieve your problem, it would be advisable for you to consult your physician or a specialist.

(A) Right hand holds Left side of neck firmly.

Left thumb presses gently upward under Right cheekbone as Left index finger holds Right forehead.

TIME: 3 minutes

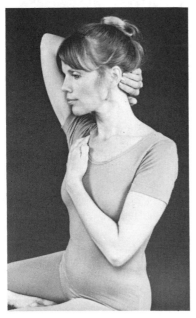

(B) Right hand presses bone behind Left ear.

Left hand presses gently upward under Right collarbone.

TIME: 3 minutes

REVERSE ROUTINE

This routine is as effective in lying position, if preferred.

eyes

Relieves pressure behind eyes and jaw tension.

Illustrated routine will help *BOTH* eyes and
BOTH sides of face.

Let mouth hang open loosely.
Press thumbs gently into jaw
hinges. Index and middle fingers
hold forehead.

TIME: 3 minutes

You may find this position more
comfortable if you rest your
elbows on a table.

*Along with many other people, I suffer tensions in my jaw.
At times, even opening my mouth is painful. This Self-
Therap/Ease routine relieves my facial tension, and relaxes
my eyes at the same time.*

FRANCES STEARNS (Transpersonal Astrologer)
Marina del Rey, Calif.

Relax Routine 58

eyes

Relaxes tired eyes. Eases problems of night vision. Relieves sinus headaches.

Illustrated routine will help *LEFT* eye.
To relieve *RIGHT* eye, follow *REVERSE ROUTINE*.

(A) Left thumb presses gently upward under Left cheekbone as Left index finger holds Left forehead.

Right thumb and index finger firmly hold Left second toe.

TIME: 3 minutes

(B) Left hand stays as in (A).

Right hand presses Left outer shoulder blade area.

TIME: 3 minutes

REVERSE ROUTINE

This routine is as effective in lying position, if preferred.

eyes

Eases eyestrain.
Relieves pressure at base of head.

Illustrated routine will help *BOTH* sides of head.

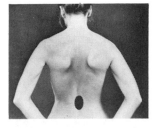

Place towel knot under spine at waist.

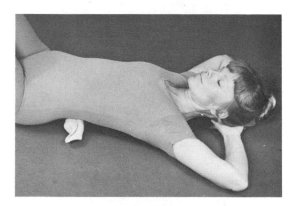

Lie on laced fingers, with thumbs pressing on Left and Right bases of skull.

TIME: 5 minutes

BACK VIEW

Illustrated to show positions of hands.

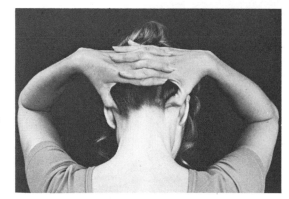

113

colds

Relieves discomforts of head colds.
Eases tightness in shoulders.

Illustrated routine will help *ENTIRE* body.

(A) Place Right hand under tailbone, palm up or down,
   whichever is more comfortable.

Left fingers press top of head.

TIME: 3 minutes

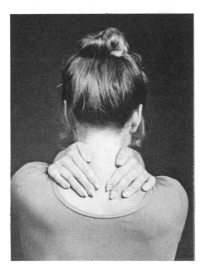

(B) Press both Right and Left
   upper shoulder blade areas.
   Cross arms if more
   comfortable.

TIME: 3 minutes

Repeat Routine four times daily
until discomforts are alleviated.

Important: Seated position helps
loosened fluids drain more easily.

colds

Relieves discomforts of head colds and sinus congestion. Helps loosen head mucus. Eases watery eye conditions.

Illustrated routine will help *RIGHT* side.
To relieve *LEFT* side, *REVERSE ROUTINE.*

Important: Seated position helps loosened fluids drain more easily.

(A) Right hand presses bone behind Left ear.

Left fingers press gently upward under Right cheekbone, close to nose.

TIME: 3 minutes

(B) Right hand stays as in (A).

Left thumb presses gently upward on bone below Right eyebrow.

TIME: 3 minutes

Repeat Routine four times daily until discomforts are alleviated.

REVERSE ROUTINE

chest

Relieves discomforts of chest colds. Loosens chest tightness and mucus. Eases stomach cramps.

Illustrated routine will help *ENTIRE* body.

(A) Cross arms comfortably. Press against inside of upper arms with thumbs of opposite hands.

TIME: 3 minutes

As a concert and choral singer, I have long had to cope with bronchial difficulties. When I asked Betty Mehling how I could help myself overcome this problem during rehearsals, she suggested this really simple procedure. By devoting these few minutes before performing — to insure cleared bronchial passages — and afterward, to remove any strain, I have found my work much easier.

MURIEL R. KRASNOW (Lyric Soprano)
Van Nuys, California

Relax Routine 63

chest

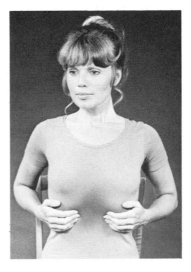

(B) Cup fingers of both hands firmly around both sides of inner rib cage.

TIME: 3 minutes

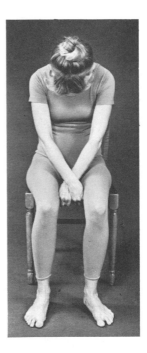

(C) Cross hands. Place fists at inner thighs, about 3 inches above knees. Press legs into your fists as hard as you can. You may find this step more comfortable, lying *on either side.*

TIME: 3 minutes

This routine is as effective in lying position, if preferred.

chest

Relieves chest colds' discomforts...bronchitis... upper arm pains...chills in shoulders.

Illustrated routine will help *LEFT* side.
To relieve *RIGHT* side, *REVERSE ROUTINE.*

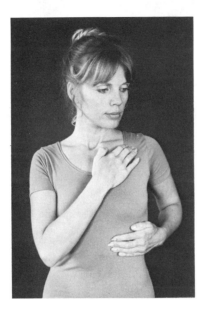

(A) Cup Left fingers firmly around Left inner rib cage.

Right fingers press gently upward under Left collarbone.

TIME: 3 minutes

I love to play bridge. Unfortunately I am allergic to tobacco fumes. Since most of my card-playing friends smoke, this used to spoil the game for me. Now that I know I will be able to relieve my chest congestion soon after I get home, I can enjoy another rubber of bridge.

CHRIS WHITE (Homemaker)
Sherman Oaks, Calif.

Relax Routine 64

chest

(B) Left hand stays as in (A).

    Right thumb presses
    Left inside upper arm.

TIME: 3 minutes

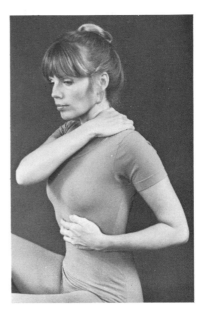

(C) Left hand stays as in (A).

    Right hand presses Left upper
    shoulder blade area.

TIME: 3 minutes

REVERSE ROUTINE

This routine is as effective
in lying position, if preferred.

coughs

Relaxes diaphragm to relieve minor coughs.

Illustrated routine will help *ENTIRE* body.

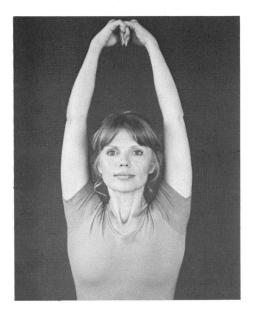

Lock fingers of both hands tightly as you stretch arms directly overhead as high as you can.

TIME: 1 minute

NOTE: If cough persists, or there are traces of blood in sputum, consult your physician at once.

With three children of elementary school age, it seemed that one or another often swallowed incorrectly and started to choke. I have shown each of them how to do this simple Self-Therap/Ease Routine. They have had remarkably good results with it, when necessary.

SALLY SHOJI (Homemaker)
Calabasas, Calif.

Relax Routine 65

coughs

Relieves coughs, tightness in throat and chest caused by colds.

Illustrated routine will help RIGHT side.
To relieve LEFT side, REVERSE ROUTINE.

If seated position is substituted, added benefits of use of towel knot would be lost.

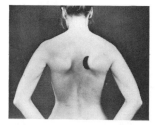

Place towel knot under Right mid-shoulder blade area.

Left hand presses gently upward under Right and Left collarbone; thumb pressing under Left side, and fingers pressing under Right side.

Cup Right fingers firmly around Right inner rib cage.

TIME: 3 minutes

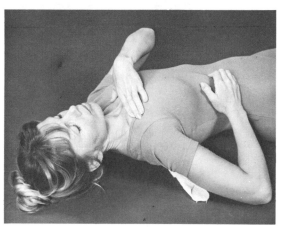

REVERSE ROUTINE AND TOWEL-KNOT POSITION.

As a waitress, I carry heavy trays. This makes my shoulders so tense that I feel as though I've been on a rack. I never go to bed without giving myself a few minutes of Self-Therap/ Ease treatment. Strange, but true, this cough routine helps me the most. By morning the soreness is gone, and I feel really rested.

ARLENE ROGERS (Waitress)

San Gabriel , Calif.

Relax Routine 66

hiccups

Eases common hiccups.
Relaxes stomach and diaphragm areas.

Illustrated routine will help *ENTIRE* body.

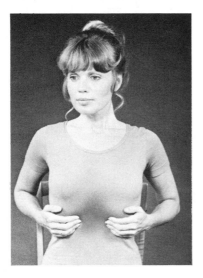

Cup fingers of both hands firmly around both sides of inner rib cage.

Breathe deeply several times.

TIME: 1 minute

Repeat every 10 minutes for one-half hour until hiccups are relieved.

As a result of a heart attack, I often have side pain from tension after work. By pressing fingers of both hands into base of my rib cage for a few minutes, I get almost immediate relief.

ROBERT GANGER (Machinist)
Sylmar, Calif.

Relax Routine 67

throat

Eases ordinary raw, dry or tight throat conditions.

Illustrated routine will help *RIGHT* side of throat.
To relieve *LEFT* side of throat, follow *REVERSE ROUTINE*.

If seated position is substituted, added benefits of use of towel knot would be lost.

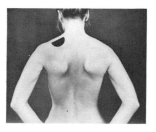

Place towel knot under Left upper shoulder blade area.

(A) Left hand holds Right inner elbow.

Right fingers press Right upper breast gently.

TIME: 3 minutes

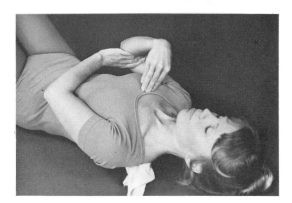

(B) Left hand stays as in (A).

Right hand holds below Left inner knee.

TIME: 3 minutes

REVERSE ROUTINE AND TOWEL-KNOT POSITION.

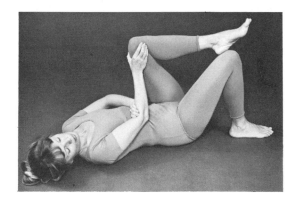

throat

Relieves many simple throat disorders...rawness caused by colds...minor swelling of neck glands... tightness caused by stress.

Illustrated routine will help *LEFT* side of throat.
To relieve *RIGHT* side of throat, follow *REVERSE ROUTINE*.

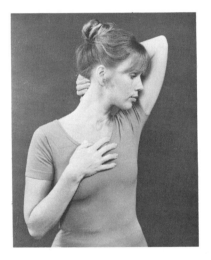

(A) Left hand presses Right base of head.

Spread Right fingers on chest, downward from Left collar-bone, so that each finger is between two ribs.

TIME: 3 minutes

This routine is equally effective in either lying or seated position.

My work often involves long hard days. My throat becomes dry and strained from continuous conversation. I have learn-ed to follow this wonderful throat-easing routine during my rest periods. Then I return to the court with my throat re-laxed and my voice refreshed.

ROSEMERY BURRWOOD (Court Interpreter)
Arleta, Calif.

Relax Routine 69

(B) Left hand stays as in (A).

    Right hand presses
Left inner thigh.

TIME: 3 minutes

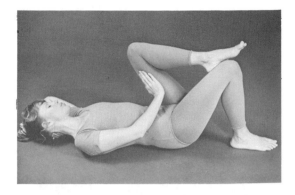

(C) Left hand stays as in (A).

    Right thumb and index finger
firmly hold Left big toe.

TIME: 3 minutes

REVERSE ROUTINE

    MAINTAIN FIRM PRESSURE. For the first few self-treatments, accumulated tensions will likely make affected areas tender to your hold. Regular use of Relax Routines will remove the sensitivity and eliminate causes of tension tenderness — *at the source.*

fevers

Helps reduce fevers and regulate body temperature. Relieves tight shoulders and pains in outer calves.

Illustrated routine will help *LEFT* side.
To relieve *RIGHT* side, *REVERSE ROUTINE.*

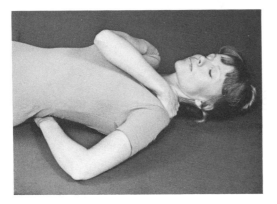

(A) Right hand presses Left upper shoulder blade area.

Place Left fist under Left waist. In seated position, leaning back into fist increases effectiveness.

TIME: 3 minutes

My body temperature seems to stay below normal. So I'm always cold. Air-conditioned movies were out of the question for me until I learned about Self-Therap/Ease skin routine. It works like a charm. You might want to try it the next time you're in a cold draft. When I don't have much time, I just use the last step (sole of foot and toe part).

GLADYS KING (Retired Teacher)
Sherman Oaks, Calif.

Relax Routine 70

(B) Right hand stays as in (A).

Left thumb presses outside upper Left calf.

TIME: 3 minutes

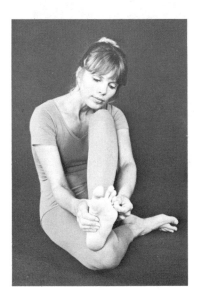

(C) Right hand holds middle bottom of Left foot.

Left thumb and index finger firmly hold Left little toe.

TIME: 3 minutes

REVERSE ROUTINE

This routine is equally effective in either lying or seated position.

NOTE: If several Self-Therap/Ease treatments, carefully selected and preceded by Relax Routine 1, do not relieve your condition, you should consult a physician.

fevers

Helps reduce fevers caused by simple disorders.
Relaxes entire body.

Illustrated routine will help *ENTIRE* body.

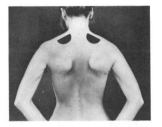

Lie on 2 towel knots,
or sponge rubber balls,
one under each upper
shoulder blade area.

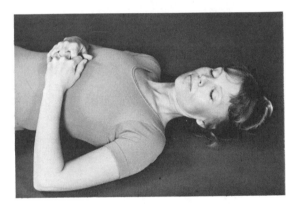

Place comfortably-laced
fingers below breasts, so that
fingertips touch body.

TIME: 5 minutes

Whenever I am restless before going to bed, I use Self-Therap/Ease as a tranquilizer. This routine never fails to soothe me to sleep naturally. It sure beats taking pills.

JACKIE GOLDBERG (Homemaker)
Chatsworth, Calif.

Relax Routine 71

menopause

Relieves hot flashes, other menopause symptoms.
Helps correct minor thyroid and hormone disorders.
Illustrated routine will help *ENTIRE* body.

Press thumbs <u>gently</u> into both sides of top of collarbone.

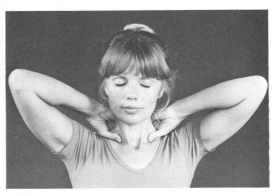

FRONT VIEW

Press fingers against both upper shoulder blade areas.

TIME: 4 minutes

This routine is as effective in lying position, if preferred.

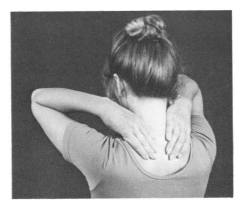

BACK VIEW

sexual

Helps relieve frigidity...impotence...
genital discomforts...menopause.
Eases groin tensions...lower backaches...tired legs.

Illustrated routine will help *LEFT* side.
To relieve *RIGHT* side, *REVERSE ROUTINE.*

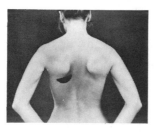

Place towel knot under Left
lower shoulder blade area.

(A) Place Right fist under Left
waist. In seated position, leaning back into fist increases
effectiveness.

Left hand presses Right
inner thigh.

TIME: 3 minutes

IF YOU NEED RELIEF on the same side (Left or Right), as
illustrated in Relax Routine, go ahead! Should your problem
be on the **other** side, REVERSE ROUTINE, as on page 26.

130

(B) Place Right hand under tailbone, palm up or down, whichever is more comfortable.

Left hand presses pubic bone.

TIME: 3 minutes

(C) Right hand stays as in (B).

Left hand presses
into Right groin.

TIME: 3 minutes

**REVERSE ROUTINE AND
TOWEL-KNOT POSITION.**

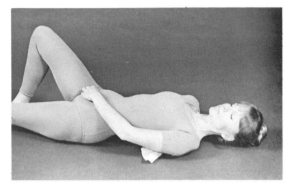

TWELVE QUICK/EASE ROUTINES,
designed for situations of limited time and
convenience, can be used at your desk or on
a bus or even in a rest room. For longer
lasting results, **Self-Therap/Ease Relax
Routines** are recommended to relieve the
conditions, in comfort at your home.

prostate

Relieves prostate and potency disorders. Eases lower backaches...general fatigue...sore feet.

Illustrated routine will help *ENTIRE* body.

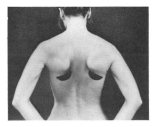

Lie on 2 towel knots, or sponge-rubber balls, under each lower shoulder blade area in (A) and (B).

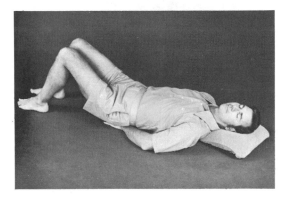

(A) Lie on hands, palms down, under back of both hips.

TIME: 3 minutes

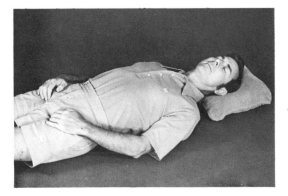

(B) Press hands firmly into Left and Right groin at same time.

TIME: 3 minutes

prostate

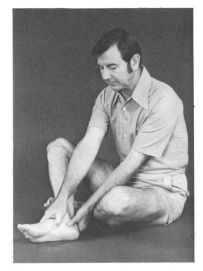

(C) Left thumb presses below inner
    Right anklebone.

    Right thumb holds outer edge
    of Right arch.

TIME: 3 minutes

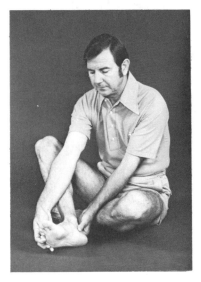

(D) Left hand stays as in (C).

    Right thumb and index finger
    firmly hold Right little toe.

TIME: 3 minutes

REPEAT (C) AND (D) ON
LEFT FOOT.

WHEN should Relax Routines be used? Whether your problem is of long duration, or you've just begun to feel it — start
Self-Therap/Ease **at once!** The sooner you start, the sooner
you'll feel results! And the less chance of the tension or ache
developing into a serious situation.

testes

Helps correct minor disorders of testes and prostate; and stimulates sexual desire.

It is important that you follow BOTH the routine illustrated AND the REVERSE ROUTINE at end of this procedure.

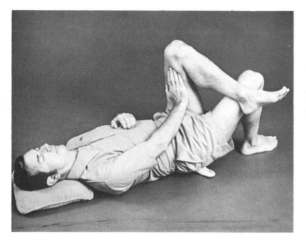

Place towel knot under spine just above tailbone.

Left hand holds base of breastbone (sternum).

Right hand presses Left inner thigh.

TIME: 3 minutes

ALWAYS REVERSE ROUTINE

FISTSFUL OF RELIEF!

If Relax Routine calls for your hands behind your back — whether you are lying down or seated — you will get relief more quickly by using your doubled-up fists, rather than the flats of your hands. Fists are especially effective when self-treatments include inner-thigh position. Any tenderness you may feel from this procedure will gradually diminish as the congestion causing the sensitivity is corrected through Self-Therap/Ease. In places awkward or uncomfortable for fists to reach, towel knot or rubber ball (explained on page 25) may be preferred.

vaginal

Eases vaginal itch. Reduces abnormal discharges.

It is important that you follow *BOTH* the routine illustrated *AND* the *REVERSE ROUTINE* at end of this procedure.

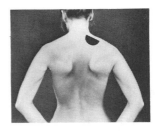

Place towel knot under Right upper shoulder blade area, next to spine.

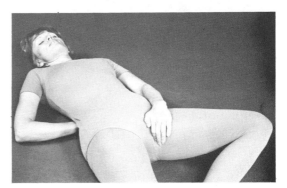

Place Right fist under Right waist.

Left hand gently presses bone at Left side of vagina.

TIME: 4 minutes

ALWAYS REVERSE ROUTINE AND TOWEL-KNOT POSITION.

Repeat twice daily until relieved. If condition is not corrected in three days, consult your physician or gynecologist.

BE SURE TO **COMBINE** placement of towel knot or ball with **positions** of your **hands,** as directed in routines where these "third hands" are included. Find the most sensitive spot within darkened areas shown on small photograph of back.

135

female

Relieves menstrual and menopause problems.
Reduces discomforts of hot flashes
...lower backaches...abdominal distress
...back-of-head pains

Illustrated routine will help *ENTIRE* body.

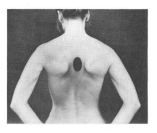

Place towel knot under spine between mid-shoulder blade areas.

(A) Cross arms comfortably. Use thumbs to press against Right and Left inside upper arms.

TIME: 3 minutes

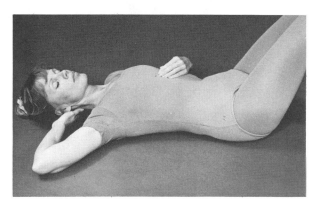

(B) Right hand presses Center base of head.

Left hand holds base of breastbone (sternum).

TIME: 3 minutes

(C) Place comfortably-laced fingers below breasts so that fingertips touch body.

TIME: 3 minutes

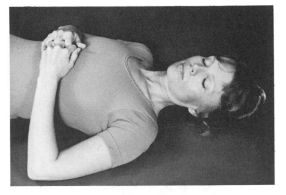

MOVE TOWEL KNOT UNDER SPINE AT WAIST.

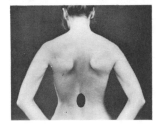

(D) Place Right hand under tail-bone, palm up or down, which-ever is more comfortable.

Left hand presses pubic bone.

TIME: 3 minutes

Repeat once daily. If you suffer difficult menstruation, follow this Routine twice daily for three days before cycle.

TIME RECOMMENDED for each step in Routines is mini-mum. Devote **as much time** as you find helpful. Self-Therap/ Ease can not harm you.

menstrual

Eases cramps caused by menstruation.
Helps relieve leg and hip pains.

Illustrated routine will help *LEFT* leg and *RIGHT* hip.
To relieve *RIGHT* leg and *LEFT* hip, follow *REVERSE ROUTINE.*

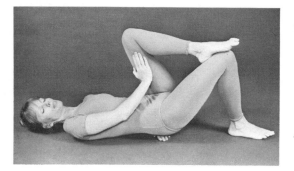

(A) Place Left hand, palm down, under back of Right hip.

Right hand presses Left inner thigh.

TIME: 3 minutes

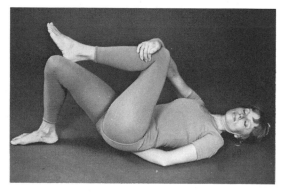

(B) Left hand stays as in (A).

Right hand holds outside upper Left calf.

TIME: 3 minutes

REVERSE ROUTINE

menstrual

**Relieves discomforts of menstruation.
Reduces pressure in large intestine.
Relaxes ovaries.**

Illustrated routine will help *LEFT* side.
To relieve *RIGHT* side, *REVERSE ROUTINE.*

(A) Place Left hand
under Left buttock.

Right hand presses
Left inner thigh.

TIME: 3 minutes

(B) Left hand stays as in (A).

Right hand presses Right
upper shoulder blade area.

TIME: 3 minutes

REVERSE ROUTINE

This routine is as effective
in lying position, if preferred.

blood

Helps correct minor blood disorders. Relieves shoulder pains. Eases discomforts in fingers.

Illustrated routine will help *LEFT* side.
To relieve *RIGHT* side, *REVERSE ROUTINE.*

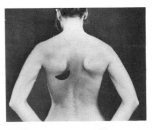

Place towel knot under Left lower shoulder blade area.

If seated position is substituted, added benefits of use of towel knot would be lost.

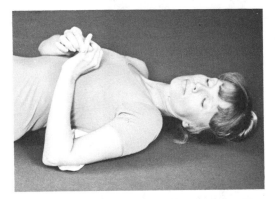

(A) Right thumb and index finger firmly hold Left fingers, below knuckle, one at a time, for one minute each.

TIME: 5 minutes

(B) Place Left fist under Left waist. In seated position, leaning back into fist increases effectiveness.

Right thumb and index finger firmly hold Right big toe.

TIME: 3 minutes

PLEASE SEE NOTE ON FACING PAGE.

REVERSE ROUTINE AND TOWEL-KNOT POSITION.

blood

Reduces problems of simple anemia.
Helps clear minor blood disturbances.
Relieves menstrual cramps.

It is important that you follow *BOTH* the routine illustrated
AND the *REVERSE ROUTINE* at end of this procedure.

(A) Place Left fist under Left waist.
In seated position, leaning back
into fist increases effectiveness.

Right thumb holds
outside upper Right calf.

TIME: 3 minutes

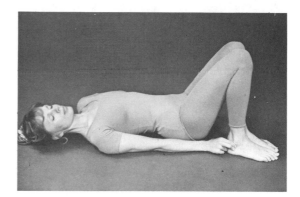

(B) Left fist stays as in (A).

Right hand presses below
outer Right anklebone.

TIME: 3 minutes

ALWAYS REVERSE ROUTINE

This routine is as effective
in seated position, if preferred.

NOTE: Please note that this routine refers
only to minor blood disorders. Please don't
try to self-diagnose a problem as vital as
your blood. Visit your doctor. Today's
laboratory procedures can analyze many
conditions through simple blood tests.

constipation

Relieves constipation. Promotes bowel regularity.

Illustrated routine will help *ENTIRE* body.

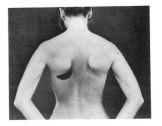

Place towel knot under Left lower shoulder blade area.

Place Right fist under Right side of tailbone.

Left hand presses Right inner thigh.

TIME: 4 minutes

NOTE: Each of us knows her or his own bodily habits better than anybody else does. Some of us are, by nature, more inclined to constipation than others are. If you feel nausea or fever or other symptoms of appendicitis; or cold sweat or acute pain, do not attempt to help yourself. Have a doctor examine you.

DO NOT REVERSE this routine. Proceed only as directed here. Depending on severity and duration of condition, this routine may be repeated daily to improve bowel functions.

*BEFORE you get out of bed in the morning, follow this simple routine for several minutes **every day,** to help relieve irregularity.*

142

diarrhea

Relieves simple diarrhea.

Illustrated routine will help *ENTIRE* body.

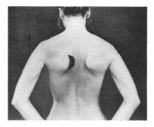

Place towel knot under Left
mid-shoulder blade area.

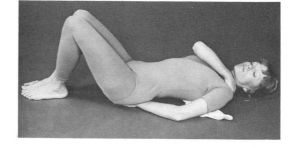

(A) Right hand presses Left
upper shoulder blade area.

Place Left hand under
back of Left hip.

TIME: 3 minutes

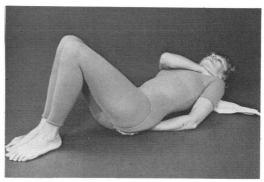

(B) Right hand stays as in (A).

Left hand holds
Left side of tailbone.

TIME: 3 minutes

DO NOT REVERSE this routine.
Proceed only as directed here.

*PLEASE SEE NOTE
ON FACING PAGE.*

hemorrhoids

Helps reduce discomforts of hemorrhoids.

Illustrated routine will help *LEFT* side.
To relieve *RIGHT* side, *REVERSE ROUTINE.*

Place towel knot under
Left side of tailbone.

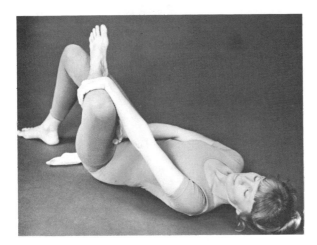

Right hand presses
Left inner thigh.

Left hand holds
outside upper Left calf.

TIME: 5 minutes

Repeat once daily until
condition improves.

**REVERSE ROUTINE AND
TOWEL-KNOT POSITION.**

SELF-THERAP/EASE is a **preventive** as well as **corrective** healing art. Self-treatments designed to relieve and control bothersome conditions should be continued **regularly.** Severe problems often require two or three repeats of Relax Routines daily until eased. After that, or in cases of mild discomforts, Self-Therap/Ease once a day will bring continued relaxation and relief of common pains.

hemorrhoids

Helps reduce hemorrhoidal discomfort.

Illustrated routine will help *BOTH* sides of body.

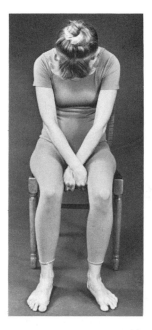

(A) Cross hands. Place fists at
    inner thighs, about 3 inches
    above knees. Press legs into
    your fists as hard as you can.
    You may find this step more
    comfortable lying,
    on either side.

TIME: 3 minutes

(B) Press both outside
    upper calves with thumbs.

TIME: 3 minutes

This routine is equally effective
in either lying or seated position.

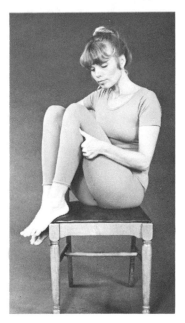

145

skin

Relieves varied skin surface disorders... itching...hives...sunburn. Helps regulate body temperature.

Illustrated routine will help *LEFT* side.
To relieve *RIGHT* side, *REVERSE ROUTINE.*

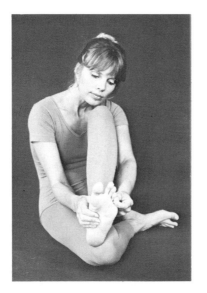

Right hand holds middle bottom of Left foot.

Left thumb and index finger firmly hold Left little toe.

TIME: 4 minutes

REVERSE ROUTINE

This routine is as effective in lying position, if preferred.

The procedure Betty Mehling showed me stopped — almost immediately — chicken pox itches in my young children. Since my daughters are only 8, 6 and 6 (twins) and they treated themselves with this routine, it is a very simple exercise indeed. This self-help really helped me out with three sick children.

JUDY MOLONEY (Hairdresser)
Woodland Hills, Calif.

Relax Routine 86

skin

Relieves many deep skin problems…complexion disorders…hot flashes…hives.
Helps regulate body temperature.
Illustrated routine will help *ENTIRE* body.

Place Right palm on Right calf.

Place Left palm on Left calf.

TIME: 4 minutes

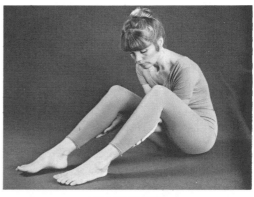

FRONT VIEW

Reverse pattern so that
arms cross and:

Right palm holds Left calf.

Left palm holds Right calf.

TIME: 4 minutes

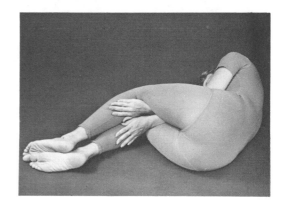

BACK VIEW

This routine is equally effective
in either lying or seated position.

facial

Relaxes premature facial lines. Brightens eyes.
Helps clear and stimulate complexion.
Eases tight scalp.

A RELAXED FACE is necessary to bring out the best of your **natural** beauty. Most strained, taut and lined features are caused by stress and fatigue. Tensions age faces prematurely. Cosmetics cannot cover these tell-tale signs.

Devoting several minutes to this easy routine — every morning and evening — will help remove the **cause** of tension marks, which add unwanted years to your appearance. The Facial Routine has been proved to restore **natural** radiance — unobtainable by make-up.

This self-treatment...regularly used... will help prevent wrinkles. There is no worthwhile substitute for the deep, inner beauty of the natural look.

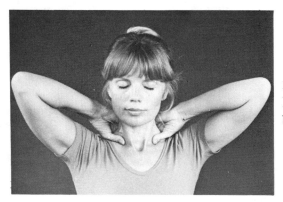

FRONT VIEW
Press thumbs <u>gently</u> into both sides of top of collarbone.

BACK VIEW
Press fingers against both upper shoulder blade areas.

TIME: 2 minutes

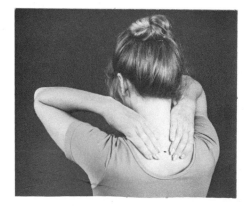

facial

Lie on laced fingers, with thumbs pressing on Left and Right bases of skull.

TIME: 2 minutes

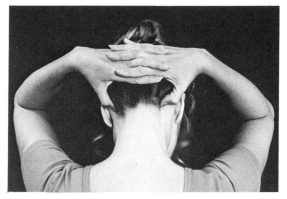

Illustrated to show positions of hands.

Let mouth hang open loosely. Press thumbs gently into jaw hinges. Index and middle fingers hold forehead.

TIME: 2 minutes

please remember....
<u>RELAX ROUTINE 1</u> *IS ALSO* **"for openers."**
*While you will find this Routine an excellent
9-minute over-all Relaxer at any time — this
procedure is especially beneficial to begin helping
your self with SELF-THERAP/EASE.*

quick/ease routines...

TWELVE QUICK/EASE ROUTINES, designed for situations of limited time and convenience, can be used at your desk or on a bus or even in a rest room. For longer-lasting results, **Self-Therap/Ease Relax Routines** are recommended to relieve the conditions, in comfort at your home.

RELAX ROUTINE 89

legs/feet

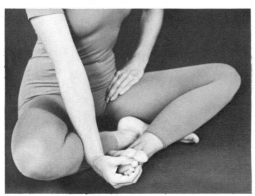

QUICK/EASE 1

Relaxes legs and feet.
(Left, as shown here.)

Left hand presses into Left groin.
Right hand holds Left toes.
(Or hold each Left toe,
one at a time, if time permits.)

TIME: 3-5 minutes

REVERSE QUICK/EASE to help Right leg/foot, if time permits.

hips

RELAX ROUTINE 90

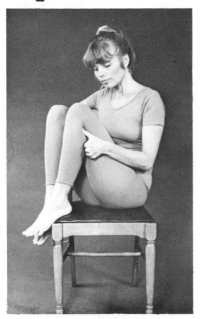

QUICK/EASE 2

Relieves hip tension.
Press both outside upper calves
with thumbs.

TIME: 3 minutes.

150

back

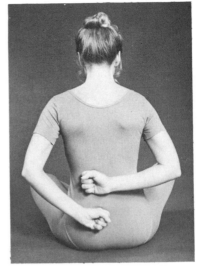

QUICK/EASE 3

Relieves backaches.

(Left, as shown here).

Place Right fist behind Left waist.

Place Left fist at back of Left hip.
Lean back into chair, or lie down.

TIME: 3 minutes

REVERSE QUICK/EASE
if time permits.

---

back/shoulder

QUICK/EASE 4

Relieves
back/shoulder tensions.

Place Right hand under
Right buttock.

Left hand presses middle of
Right shoulder blade.

TIME: 3 minutes

REVERSE QUICK/EASE
if time permits.

stomach

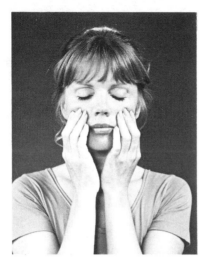

QUICK/EASE 5

Relieves upset stomach.

Press gently upward
under both cheekbones.

TIME: 3 minutes

---

constipation

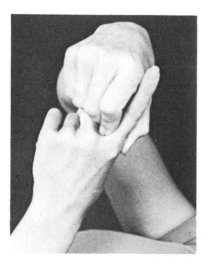

QUICK/EASE 6

Relieves constipation.

Use Right thumb to hold inside of
Left index finger firmly.
Work length of finger, holding for
a minute, between each joint.

TIME: 3 minutes

REVERSE QUICK/EASE
if time permits.

coughs

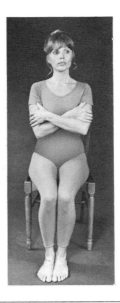

QUICK/EASE 7

Relieves cigarette cough.

Cross arms comfortably.
Press against inside of upper arms
with thumbs of opposite hands.

TIME: 3 minutes

---

shoulders

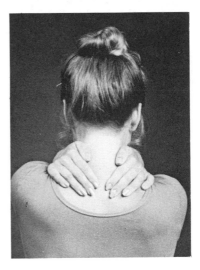

QUICK/EASE 8

Relieves shoulder tensions.

Press both Right and Left upper
shoulder blade areas.
Cross arms, if more comfortable.

TIME: 3 minutes

eyes

QUICK/EASE 9

Relaxes tired eyes.

Place thumbs on bone below eyebrows, close to bridge of nose, and press upward gently.

TIME: 3 minutes

---

eyes/head

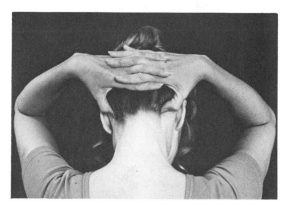

QUICK/EASE 10

Relieves eye-tension/headaches.

Lace fingers behind head, with thumbs pressing on Left and Right bases of skull.

TIME: 5 minutes

head

QUICK/EASE 11

Relieves simple headaches.

Place Left hand across forehead,
applying firm pressure with palm
and fingertips.

Right hand presses Left base
of head.

TIME: 3 minutes

REVERSE QUICK/EASE
if time permits.

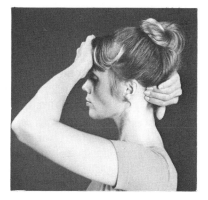

---

sinus

QUICK/EASE 12

Relieves sinus pressure.

(Right, as shown here).

Right hand presses bone behind
Left ear.

Left fingers press gently upward
under Right cheekbone,
close to nose.

TIME: 3 minutes

REVERSE QUICK/EASE
if time permits.

about the authors

Bonnie Pendleton began her long involvement with Oriental therapy in her late twenties. That was shortly after authentic Asiatic natural healing was introduced to this country in California in the mid-1950s.

A few months earlier, her husband, Douglas, had suffered an aneurism in his leg—rare for one just past 30. An artery transplant was performed. Following surgery, circulation in his leg was impaired. Conventional therapy proved to be of limited help, and the doctors offered no further recommendations other than additional surgery.

By coincidence, Bonnie was told of a Japanese family, the Iino's, who recently moved to Southern California. The daughter, Mary, was skilled in Oriental healing. She had studied under Dr. Jiro Murai, who for over 50 years had been the outstanding authority in the Far East on this natural therapy. For more than 20 years, Mary Iino has been the most capable and dedicated practitioner of Asiatic healing arts in America.

After several sessions with Mary, Douglas Pendleton's condition improved tremendously. Bonnie asked if she could help speed her husband's recovery by using home treatments between sessions at the Iino's. Mary explained a few simple routines. These worked well.

Bonnie was fascinated by this experience and wondered whether she too could use her hands to help others in need. She asked Mary if she could assist in minor phases of this art and served a conscientious apprenticeship—practicing, observing, studying, and understanding more every day. For several years, Bonnie was associated as a fellow practitioner of Mary Iino.

Thus, Bonnie Pendleton became the first American practitioner fully trained in America in authentic Oriental therapy by the most qualified specialist of Healing by Hand in this country.

When her associate left California because of family duty, Mrs. Pendleton continued practicing and teaching. In the past few years, she has lectured on Therap/Ease—the simplified routines she has developed in conjunction with Betty Mehling—before many groups, including hospital physical therapy departments. She has appeared as a featured guest on television programs—both national and local—demonstrating Therap/Ease.

Combining Bonnie's longer experience in therapy with Betty's training in journalism produced the best-known team of authors in this field. In 1974, between treating those in need of relief from varied tensions and Bonnie's teaching duties, they collaborated in producing a textbook for advanced students. This book is currently in classroom use. In 1975 and 1976, Betty Mehling and Bonnie Pendleton were the only Healing by Hand practitioners invited to participate in the Headache Seminars at The University of California at Los Angeles Medical Center.

At present, Bonnie Pendleton is busy arranging classroom courses in Self-Therap/Ease, with Relax Routines **combined** to relieve specific and chronic problems. She is also working with Betty Mehling on plans for their next book, *Helping Others for the Health of It.*

Betty Mehling never would have met Bonnie Pendleton if she hadn't been waiting in her car for a traffic light to change when the driver behind forgot to stop for a red light.

The rear-end impact started a long series of sickening headaches and depressing side effects for Betty, who was then a high school journalism teacher. She was dosed with pain-dulling drugs that were gradually increased in strength and spent countless hours in traction, both in and out of hospitals. When she accompanied her Air Force Reservist husband on two years' camp duty, she spent much of the time in the office of the chief neurologist and in the physical therapy department of the base hospital.

When she returned to California, she seemed to be kept going by pills. In her early twenties, she felt that this suffering would always be part of her life. Friends who had been relieved of disabling conditions by Asiatic natural healing urged her to try this method. Because of limited relief obtained from sophisticated physical therapy equipment, she was reluctant at first to experiment with foreign ideas. But she wearily consented to try this different approach.

Within a relatively short time, Mary and Bonnie had ended Betty's three years of severe headaches. Restoring and maintaining the natural balance of bodily flows had brought lasting relief. Every day Betty used self-treatments, taught her by Bonnie, to remove tensions. These routines stopped the headaches at their source—muscles affected by stress.

As the experience relieved Betty Mehling physically, it renewed her energy at the same time. And it invigorated her mentally. She was inspired to learn more of this Far Eastern art. This procedure had succeeded with her where years of conventional Western methods and medication had failed. Her interest grew from journalist's questions to firm belief in this technique—old in practice, yet always renewing well-being. She felt that this career would offer her much more personal satisfaction than her editorial position with a major newspaper. She earnestly studied and passed beginner's, advanced, and instructor's courses. In addition, she read all the material she could find on Asiatic Healing by Hand and related techniques. Prior to 1972, books on these subjects were scarce in this country.

Betty Mehling's interest in further knowledge led to many discussions with Bonnie Pendleton. They found that they shared progressive thoughts in making Oriental healing arts easier for Americans to understand. Together, they developed Westernized adaptations of authentic techniques, to be known as Therap/Ease.

The authors may be reached through Therap/Ease, Inc., Box 8417, Calabasas, CA 91302.

future therap/easers...

JUST AS **PROPER COMBINATIONS** of hand-holds, based on authentic Asiatic healing techniques, alleviate common tensions ...**combinations** of **Relax Routines,** in correct sequence, can relieve many out-of-the-ordinary or more severe conditions. The authors are now working on series of these sequences, which will be available in inexpensive booklet format, as companion self-helps to RELAX! WITH SELF-THERAP/EASE. The booklet will be devoted entirely to methods of removing deeply-rooted tensions through combinations of Relax Routines.

AS WIVES AND MOTHERS, Bonnie Pendleton and Betty Mehling have also been developing a series of Family Therap/Ease Routines. These patterns are being designed to help parents ease discomforts and minor physical problems of children — and other members of families — by use of authentic natural healing methods. Among routines devised and tested are the four illustrated here.

Reduces fever. Relieves shoulder tension, arm fatigue.

Helps ease hives, discomforts of chicken pox, measles. Clears complexion.

Alleviates stomach upsets.

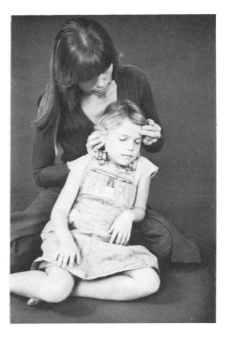

General relaxer. Relieves headaches, sinus discomforts, head colds.

Two young boys and 11 hours at Disneyland added up to TIRED LEGS and WOUND-UP SPIRITS. Within minutes after starting a recommended Therap/Ease routine on each of them, they began to relax. Soon they fell asleep peacefully. Their legs didn't ache the next day.

SALLY JIMINEZ
North Hollywood, Calif.

My sister, brother and I were raised on Therap/Ease. Because our mom, Bonnie Pendleton, always cared for us, I never learned to work on myself until I married. Now I use Self-Therap/Ease to stay healthy. My son is a Therap/

Ease baby. When he was just a few weeks old, he suffered colic. I placed my fingers on his tiny inner thighs. Soon, his tummy would gurgle and he would be peacefully asleep.

DEBORAH PENDLETON TREPP
Monterey Park, Calif.

I first used Therap/Ease on somebody else when my 12-year-old son came home from school with a high temperature. After five minutes of this procedure his fever was gone. He felt so much better it was hard to believe. Now he tells all his friends his mother is a *healer*...thanks to Therap/Ease.

JACKIE GOLDBERG
Chatsworth, Calif.

159

in appreciation

The authors are grateful for the complete cooperation of two professional friends. These two—highly respected in their fields—have contributed much skill, talent, and effort to make the Relax Routine pages pleasant to read and easy to understand.

Our lovely model, **Marta Kristen,** has appeared often on television, in movies, in magazine advertising, and in stage performances. Marta's screen credits include leading roles in Walt Disney's *Savage Sam* and *Once,* which merited an official invitation to the 1974 Cannes Film Festival. For three years, Marta was featured in the TV series, *Lost in Space.* She also has performed on many other TV shows, as well as in commercials, films, live theater, and modeling.

During many tedious hours needed to pose precisely in recording more than 250 self-relief positions, Marta used Self-Therap/Ease treatments to keep herself relaxed. She says that she finds these procedures helpful in keeping herself fit and calm during the otherwise frustrating waits between takes in her performing arts work. Presently, Marta lives in Santa Monica, California, with her daughter Lora, who posed as the child model on the preceding pages, and her husband, Kevin.

The name of **Kathleen Ballard**—the woman behind the camera that effectively captured all the steps in *Relax! with Self-Therap/Ease*—has been seen in print, under photos she has taken, by millions of Californians. Kathleen, a member of the Board of the Greater Los Angeles Press Photographers Association, has been credited with hundreds of dramatic and interesting newsphotos. She is possibly best known for her inspired photos of children in varying moods and expressions, which have won awards for her. As a sports enthusiast, Kathleen Ballard is also familiar with the advantages of Self-Therap/Ease—especially during and after her favorite outdoor activities, sailing and snow skiing. She knows how to ease her muscle strains naturally. Kathleen lives with her husband, Tim, and their son, Tommy, in Friday Harbor, Washington.

to feel better, sooner...

please... FOLLOW THESE INSTRUCTIONS **BEFORE** YOU SELECT ROUTINE!

CONDITIONS RELIEVED BY SELF-THERAP/EASE are alphabetically indexed.

BOLD-TYPE page numbers show Relax Routines designed to relieve **specific** conditions. Although some problems included in **bold-type** figures may not be listed on the Routine numbered, the self-treatments recommended are also effective in easing conditions indexed.

BEFORE YOU START TREATING YOURSELF, you are **urged** to **please** read **all bold-type** listings on **all** pages in which your problem is covered, as numbered in Index. You can thus pick the **right** Relax Routines, carefully planned to relieve **you** most effectively. Relax Routines in light-type page numbers alleviate similar conditions, and may also be helpful in your case.

ALSO, KEEP IN MIND that **Self**-Therap/Ease is a **supplementary** therapy — **not** a substitute for attention by a physician, or a qualified practitioner of Therap/Ease.

AND REMEMBER, EVERY BODY IS DIFFERENT. Allow for variations when you select Routines!

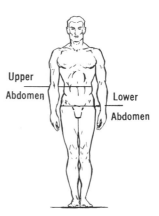

Upper Abdomen — Lower Abdomen

for speedy relief... QUICK/EASE Routine number
is designated (in parenthesis) after page number,

for speedy relief... QUICK/EASE Routine number
is designated (in parenthesis) after page number,

for speedy relief... QUICK/EASE Routine number
is designated (in parenthesis) after page number,

*for speedy relief...*QUICK/EASE Routine number
is designated (in parenthesis) after page number,

*for speedy relief...*QUICK/EASE Routine number
is designated (in parenthesis) after page number,

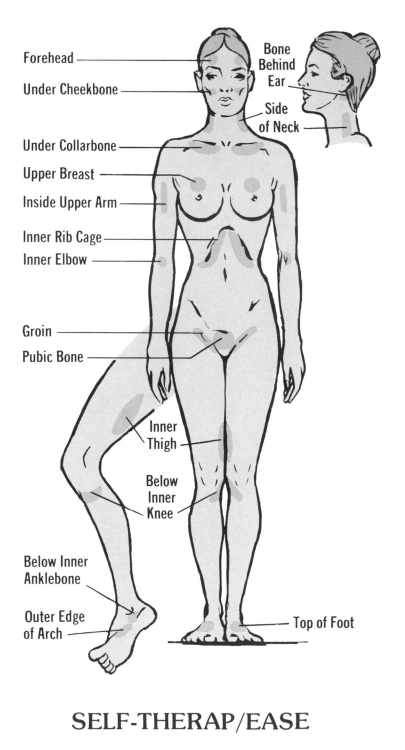

Forehead

Under Cheekbone

Under Collarbone

Upper Breast

Inside Upper Arm

Inner Rib Cage

Inner Elbow

Groin

Pubic Bone

Inner Thigh

Below Inner Knee

Below Inner Anklebone

Outer Edge of Arch

Bone Behind Ear

Side of Neck

Top of Foot

SELF-THERAP/EASE

POWER CENTERS

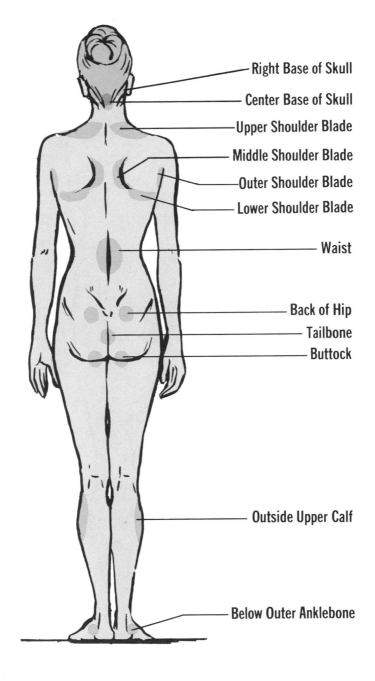

Right Base of Skull

Center Base of Skull

Upper Shoulder Blade

Middle Shoulder Blade

Outer Shoulder Blade

Lower Shoulder Blade

Waist

Back of Hip

Tailbone

Buttock

Outside Upper Calf

Below Outer Anklebone

SELF-THERAP/EASE
POWER CENTERS

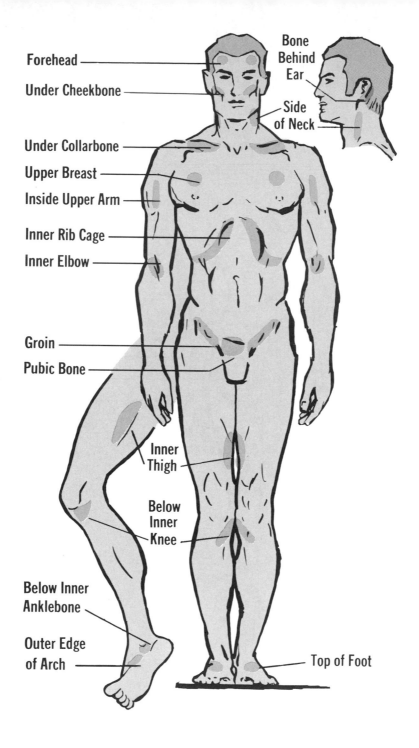

Forehead

Bone Behind Ear

Under Cheekbone

Side of Neck

Under Collarbone

Upper Breast

Inside Upper Arm

Inner Rib Cage

Inner Elbow

Groin

Pubic Bone

Inner Thigh

Below Inner Knee

Below Inner Anklebone

Outer Edge of Arch

Top of Foot

SELF-THERAP/EASE

POWER CENTERS

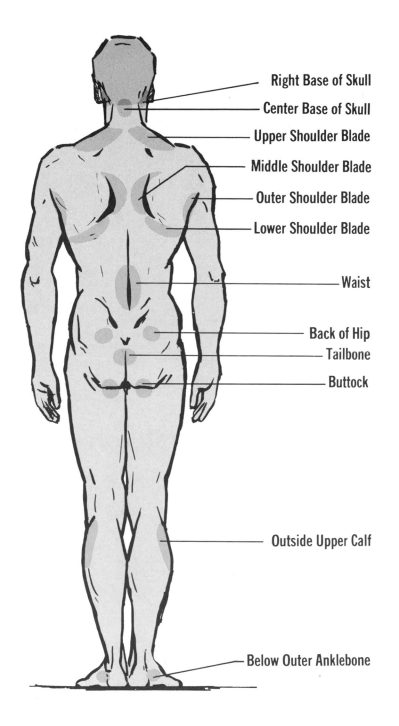

- Right Base of Skull
- Center Base of Skull
- Upper Shoulder Blade
- Middle Shoulder Blade
- Outer Shoulder Blade
- Lower Shoulder Blade
- Waist
- Back of Hip
- Tailbone
- Buttock
- Outside Upper Calf
- Below Outer Anklebone

SELF-THERAP/EASE

POWER CENTERS